Inside Grey's Anatomy:

The Unauthorized Biography of Jamie Dornan

New York Times
Best-selling Author

Marc Shapiro

Inside Grey's Anatomy: The Unauthorized Biography of Jamie Dornan© 2014 by Marc Shapiro

All Rights Reserved. No part of this book may be reproduced or transmitted in any form or by any means, electronic or mechanical, including photocopying, without permission in writing from the publisher.

For more information contact:
Riverdale Avenue Books
5676 Riverdale Avenue
Riverdale, NY 10471.

www.riverdaleavebooks.com

Design by www.formatting4U.com
Cover by Scott Carpenter

Digital ISBN 9781626011564
Print ISBN 9781626011571

First Edition February 2015

THIS BOOK IS DEDICATED TO...

The never ending support, encouragement and love of my wife Nancy. My daughter Rachael whose life has been a constant and loving example of what it is to be a father. My granddaughter Lily who reminds me constantly of the importance of play. My agent Lori Perkins. It's been a long time and it's been time well spent. Mike from back in the day and the here and now. Brady and Mr. Fitch. Good dogs. The real people who do the real work. And finally to those who take the changes out on the edge of life and form a creative legacy against all odds. Welcome Jamie Dornan as the newest member of the club.

TABLE OF CONTENTS

AUTHOR'S NOTES…AN INTERESTING CAT	i
INTRODUCTION: STORAGE WARS TO FIFTY SHADES	1
ONE…DAD DELIVERS BABIES	11
TWO…SHORT, CUTE AND BLOODY	16
THREE…TROUBLES	21
FOUR…MODEL CITIZEN	27
FIVE…DORNAN GOES KNIGHTLEY	35
SIX…JAMIE'S CALVINS	42
SEVEN…POP GOES JAMIE	52
EIGHT…OPEN SEASON	59
NINE…AFTER A FEW DRINKS	64
TEN…HOT AND HUMILIATING	71
ELEVEN…AND THEN YOU DIE	76
TWELVE…ALL FALL	83
THIRTEEN…JAMIE'S IN LOVE	93
FOURTEEN…TWO FOR THE SHOW	97
FIFTEEN…ONE AND ONE MAKE THREE	103
SIXTEEN…WALK LIKE A GREY	110
SEVENTEEN…FIRST DAYS ON FIFTY	117
EIGHTEEN…SEX…ISN'T IT ROMANTIC?	125
NINETEEN…FALLOUT	129
TWENTY…RESHOOT	138
TWENTY ONE…NOW YOU SEE IT	145
FILMOGRAPHY	151
DISCOGRAPHY	151
SOURCES	153
MORE BOOKS	155
AUTHOR'S NOTES	157

AN INTERESTING CAT

The word 'unknown' can mean many things.

There is the connotation of a mystery, a person, place or thing that is a literal blank slate. A line once crossed into a situation where there is no turning back. When it comes to actors and Hollywood, the word 'unknown' can spell both risk and reward.

Which is pretty much the part of the equation in which Jamie Dornan dwells.

Jumping immediately from the biography of *Fifty Shades of Grey's* leading lady Dakota Johnson to her male co-star Jamie Dornan seemed at first to be the ultimate exercise in relentless research and making a mountain out of a mole hill. Dakota was known for doing a lot of work, most of which was barely seen, being the offspring of two celebrities and suddenly bursting into the public's consciousness when chosen to play Anastasia Steele.

Done and done.

Going straight into *Inside Grey's Anatomy: The Unauthorized Biography of Jamie Dornan*, quite honestly, seemed like a burnout in the making. Because, like Dakota, Jamie was known and not known in the same breath. If you're a groupie of the fashion/ modeling scene, you might have seen Dornan, who in the day was described as 'The Golden Torso,' stripped down to his underwear on massive outdoor billboards in many major cities and on the sides of just as many buses. If you were a geek for British folk music, you might have been there for the moment in time when he was one half of the short-lived folk duo, Sons of Jim, who made a small and short-lived splash across the pond. And finally, if you get all moist at the thought of British cult movies and television, you might have captured the all-important glimpse of Dornan as the quite uncommon model-turned-actor who could actually act in the likes of *Marie Antoniette, Once Upon A Time* and *The Fall*.

That Jamie could boast even a moderate level of acting credits after nearly a decade in the modeling trenches could be chalked up as amazing. With the rare exception, highlighted by model turned actor George Lazenby's turn as James Bond in *On Her Majesties Secret Service* (one of the most underappreciated Bond film portrayals to date), most models have carried the idea of transitioning to acting to often-laughable ends. But from the beginning, Jamie has not been most models. He wanted to be an actor long before he took his clothes off for Calvin Klein. In the most thoughtful and mercenary sense, Jamie had turned to modeling to turn a buck and travel the world.

But resumes are not ultimately what full blown biographies are made of and what makes Jamie's story all the more attractive is that he is not a paper-thin sum of his credits but rather a flesh and blood Shakespeare done up with 70's New Wave European cool, alternately shy and introspective, rugged and stereotypically one of the boys and seemingly always passionately determined. Jamie loves to read the works of Oscar Wilde, is a big fan of both The Kinks and The Smiths and is notorious for dropping a requisite amount of F bombs into just about any conversation he's having. He plays a man's sport, rugby, and can be a notoriously hard drinker; sure signs that he has testosterone as well as sensitivity running through his veins.

Physically he's every man and don't let that Adonis of a model's torso fool you. He's had his nose broken three times over the years and one of those was the result of a bar fight. He suffered a shoulder injury on the rugby pitch that continues to bother him on occasion. And he makes no bones about the fact that he's had asthma forever and jokes that his constant companion, an asthma pump, is the ultimate cool bobble.

While the flesh and blood model of style and elegance, at the end of the day Jamie is very much of his Irish upbringing, equal parts blue collar and salt of the earth and, as he once explained to *ASOS Magazine*, he was a man of simple tastes, his dream to have three nice shirts, two nice pair of trousers and three T-shirts. He also offered that his simple tastes run to Sky Sports (a sports television network), Guinness beer and burgers.

That so much is actually known about Jamie Dornan can be chalked up to a combination of the press, often unabashedly and kind of pervy, attraction to his classic features and the fact that Jamie, despite being prone to privacy, although not in a Garbo-esque sense, will spill the beans with surprising frequency, at least to the extent that he wants to.

But get into his inner circle, one populated by a mixture of old school mates, actors and a sprinkling of fashion people, and one is reportedly likely to see a much softer man. He has admitted that, in his less guarded moments, that he is prone to being extremely open when it comes to personal matters. And, on a much more intimate level, he has been known to cry. Depth and emotion does not grow on trees. Like I said, Jamie Dornan is one interesting cat.

Just who Jamie's heavy friends are is open to conjecture. His modeling and acting days had obviously put him in contact with celebrity notables but Jamie has never been one to name drop. In fact if it had not been for a recent interview, nobody would have known that Jamie considered actor Josh Hartnett a great friend. This is how Jamie operates. Just when you think you've gotten it all, the actor decides to drop another tidbit.

In researching Jamie's story, I found an almost kinetic energy pulsating through even the most day to day moments. An urgency and a drive that makes Jamie constantly bordering, physically and emotionally, on larger than life. Things have not just happened in his life and career. There's a mixture of luck and karma to be considered. But what it all boils down to is a sudden jolt in his world and Jamie is on the scene.

Jamie is seemingly impervious to pain. When a painful shoulder injury, acquired on the rugby pitch, necessitated surgery, Jamie put off the procedure for three years, preferring to walk around with the discomfort. By model standards, he's been roughed up with several broken noses, which has made him the enticing contrary to the pretty boy face, attractive yet slightly out of symmetry with the concept of male beauty.

There's been trauma in his life which is always an important element of a good celebrity biography. And no, I am not a cold-hearted bastard. It's just that real life often throws the dice that way and how Jamie reacted to the death of his mother and the death of four close friends is part of the equation.

Jamie's love life immediately jumps out of the time line. Quite simply, you do not look like Jamie Dornan and not always have the eye of the ladies. His two year relationship with then model/actress and later major movie star Kiera Knightly is definitely of note just because we want to know what happens when two people who are physically beyond belief get together. The fact that he made Lindsay Lohan's 'I had sex with' list is amusing and, for purposes of this tome, puts Jamie in elite (sic) company. It is hard to imagine Jamie as a paper-thin sex machine. My guess is that even Lindsay got more than she bargained for.

Okay. Sensation. It's a celebrity biography. You knew those things were coming.

But Jamie is a much deeper subject than your normal flavor of the moment, those flash in the pans whose career barely outlasts pop culture's fleeting fascination with them. Jamie Dornan is definitely a different cat. Who has the potential to be around for awhile.

He is a thinker equally at home alone with his thoughts than in a crowd or in front of a camera. There is a soul and a very real one nestled inside his sculpted body and often shy good looks. There is a brain and a functioning one as well which is constantly working, calculating the right move in the right situation, even as he parlayed coming in second to Charlie Hunnam in the Christian Grey sweepstakes.

Many would panic in suddenly being rejected and out of work. Jamie did not. There was a loving wife and a newborn child to consider, the prospect of returning to the second season of the hit UK television series *The Fall*. Hell Jamie was so much the perfect bloke that even a television series that had killed him off was, a year earlier, was still moving heaven and earth trying to think of a way to bring his character back and make it work within his currently always hectic schedule.

Nothing in Jamie's life seems to just lay there inert. There always seems to be a sense of impeding something as he makes his way through the day. But you can be sure that Jamie has worked very hard and has been diligent in making his life and career what it is today.

If you've read this far, then I guess I've done my job. Which is to get you to read the rest. *Inside Grey's Anatomy: The Unauthorized Biography of Jamie Dornan* is in your face primarily because of his ascendency to the role of Christian Grey.

Lest you forget, this is how the pop culture biography writing game works. Somebody rises to popularity in the media and in the public consciousness. A book is written for the purpose of engaging, enlightening and entertaining the reader. Yes the author pays his mortgage, the publisher is happy and everybody lives happily ever after.

Make no mistake, *Inside Grey's Anatomy: The*

Unauthorized Biography of Jamie Dornan is not just a whole lot of fluff and filler about Jamie Dornan and *Fifty Shades*. You would be disappointed if his current role was the only thing worth reading about.

And so would Jamie.

With the conclusion of *Inside Grey's Anatomy: The Unauthorized Biography of Jamie Dornan*, I have now written three books on the subject, four if you count the additional chapters for the updated version of my book on E. L. James.

I think I've pretty much covered it.

But this is publishing and this is show business. So you never really know.

Marc Shapiro 2015

INTRODUCTION
STORAGE WARS TO FIFTY SHADES

2:00 a.m. London. Late October 2013. Jamie is alone in the dark.

Well, not exactly alone.

Flickering on his television are the figures of working-class Americans bidding frantically and hilariously on the contents of storage units. The program, a US import reality show entitled *Storage Wars*, has a strange effect after repeated viewings, alternately hypnotic and heavy on the brain. A show that easily melts into mental background noise after predictability and repeated viewings and allows the mind to wander. Jamie was on his umpteenth episode of the show that had started well before midnight and it was having what was for him a desired effect.

Jamie in repose does not suit him well. Long addicted to physical activity, the idea of sitting around and not doing push-ups, non-stop pacing or other activities often gives him the mental shakes after a time. Just ask his wife, Amelia, who has regularly admonished him, as he explained in an *Observer* interview, to stop dropping to the floor to do spontaneous exercises and to just read a book.

Jamie's eyes moved back and forth from the screen, a glazed, sleep-deprived look. The television was turned down low in difference to his pregnant wife Amelia who was sleeping soundly downstairs. He was dressed comfortably in pajamas that hung easily on a lean lanky frame. But even in the late hour, Jamie was most certainly contemplative and, yes, a bit brooding. It was a look that close friends and business acquaintances had known for some time. Jamie was reportedly anxious and excited and was in a pensive state. He regularly stared at the phone gripped tightly in his hand.

It was a death grip.

"I was in London," Jamie recalled that night in an interview with *Today*. "It was 2:00 a.m. I was waiting for the call."

The call that just might change his life forever.

2013 had been an eventful year for Jamie. After years of struggling to shake off the profitable but creatively unsatisfying shackles of top international modeling, and after posing in various stages of undress for high fashion icons, he was heartened by the notion that his long hoped for acting career was finally beginning to take off.

He had garnered particular praise in the role of Abel Goffe in the multi-part historical drama *New Worlds*, a sequel to the previous mini-series *Devil's Whore*. And his turn as the truly terrifying serial killer Paul Spector in the UK produced thriller television series *The Fall*, opposite *X-Files* stalwart Gillian Anderson, had been so successful that, as he lounged around watching *Storage Wars*, the show had already been renewed for a second season and he was contemplating his return as what viewers had noted was the sexiest killer on the planet sometime in the new year.

That Jamie had come so far seemingly so fast did not come as a surprise to his father, Dr. Jim Dornan who, in an *Irish Central* story, made no bones about the fact that, all parental bias aside, his son was first rate. "He is an incredibly level-headed, solid guy. He is one of the nicest people I know."

And it was this sense of normalcy and nonchalance that had become an early trademark of the model turned actor. Jamie had never been one to put on airs, being more content to just be one of the group and to go about his business of doing the work. The notion that, with success, he might suddenly evolve into an ego driven diva, had not come to pass. He has often had a good laugh at the notion of how boring he must appear to those seeking celebrity flash and glitz and, in a conversation with *Glamour Poland*, he was laughingly quick to outline just how much of an anti-celebrity he actually was.

"I despise extravagance," he chuckled. "I don't fly a private plane. I don't have a bodyguard. I don't buy brand name stuff. I have a house, a family, two dogs and a watch. That's good enough for me."

In the ensuing years his lack of diva-ish tendencies and laidback attitude had become part and parcel of any conversation about what it was like working with him.

Typical of this were the comments of actress Bronagh Waugh who plays Jamie's wife in *The Fall*. "He's just Jamie," the actress told *In!*. "It's just a work thing. The interest in him is weird. I went for an audition once and I think the only reason I was called was that I had worked with Jamie."

But even as he contemplated a bright professional future, the working class in Jamie, one that in conversation was highlighted by a classic Irish brogue, could not help but remember how difficult it had been not that many years ago. The countless auditions, the just as many rejections and, as he ruefully explained in an interview with *Red Magazine,* the never-ending preconceived notions that any model turned aspiring actor must deal with.

"In Los Angeles they don't think that because you leaned against a wall and looked depressed while someone took your photograph, it just means you can't act. In the UK there's a massive stigma attached to it. You could not have possibly had your photograph taken for a living and act."

But the changes in Jamie's life have been equally personal. After years of being considered the sexiest man in the modeling world and carrying on relationships with such equally attractive modeling icons as Kiera Knightly and, allegedly Kate Moss and, at the other extreme, allegedly a brief sexual encounter with Lindsay Lohan, Jamie, at age 31, has seen a more mature side emerge in his marriage to actress/musician Amelia Warner and the impending birth of their first child.

Jamie was comfortable with his new state of maturity and bliss when he talked to *Entertainment Weekly*. "I feel very settled. I'm glad to be 31 and not 21. I'm not running in and out of clubs at 5:00 a.m. anymore."

Sometime in the early morning hours the phone in Jamie's hand suddenly vibrated.

Jamie had been well aware of everything *Fifty Shades of Grey*. He knew the trio of books had captivated the imaginations of hundreds of millions of women worldwide. He was aware that a movie deal had been struck and he was also aware that the hunt for just the right actor to play kinky millionaire Christian Grey was being carried on in earnest and on an international scale. Instinctively he knew the career making possibilities of the role and had reportedly been mildly interested in auditioning. Midway through the year, and at the suggestion of his agency representatives, Jamie submitted a video tape audition for the role.

Jamie was well aware of the history of the *Fifty Shades of Grey* books, how the middle-aged housewife E.L James had dropped out of the figurative sky to become the pioneer of modern erotica. He knew that a lot of money had already been thrown into the hopper and that the actors involved would certainly become instant celebrities. Jamie had kept his *Fifty Shades* submission largely low key. From the word go, his family and friends were curious but ultimately supportive. His mates from back in the day had some good natured laughs at his expense but were. Likewise, enthusiastic.

These were manic times in the hunt for Christian Grey. *Fifty Shades* fanatics were suggesting, and yes, demanding their personal favorites be chosen. Author E.L. James was very vocal in her suggestions. And of course the studio and producers had a shortlist of their own. All of which circled a start time for the film that was fairly set in stone.

While the particulars of the process are not well

known, what was known was that whoever made the final cut would have to audition with and have the proper chemistry with the actress who would play Anastasia Steele, Dakota Johnson. What is known is that there was a heavy UK influence in the finalists. Jamie and fellow Brit Christian Cooke were considered legitimate contenders. Others who were being considered were Alexander Skarsgard, Billy Magnussen, Scott Eastwood (son of Clint) and a real dark horse by the name of Luke Bracy. As was another actor from across the pond, Charlie Hunnam, who had come to the attention of audiences through his long run on the US biker series *Sons of Anarchy*.

Searching for the perfect Christian would not be easy for any number of reasons. Many names would be floated for consideration. According to a report in *The Hollywood Reporter*, highest on the list was Ryan Gosling who, on paper, was considered the perfect match for the kinky businessman. Gosling was not interested. Reportedly running a close second was Garrett Hedlund who was heavily courted before he finally turned the offer down on the grounds that he did not feel he could connect with the character.

Although nobody was coming right out and saying so, the fate of another notorious film, *Showgirls*, was definitely haunting the search. Elizabeth Berkeley's career had been dealt a heavy blow, one she has yet to even remotely recover from and many were reluctant to take on the role in *Fifty Shades* which, many were speculating, could become the new Showgirls.

And so the hunt continued.

David Gandy, an actor who had early on been

suggested for the role of Christian but had declined because he felt the source material was badly written, explained in a *50 Shades* blog, that Jamie was his personal favorite for the role. "It's something that Jamie wants and I'm a lot shyer than him about things. He's a musician and he's gone out with very famous women. He's much more comfortable in that whereas I'm much more secretive."

But those plusses aside, Jamie was considered a long shot at best. Despite some success and no small amount of notoriety, that old bugaboo of being a model continued to cast doubt in the decision maker's eyes. While *The Fall* had made him a minor celebrity internationally and his brief stint in *Once Upon A Time* had generated some fan heat, he was considered just too much of a question mark and risk for a production that had a lot of money and reputations hanging in the balance.

And it would ultimately boil down name recognition that carried the day when, on September 2, 2013, it was announced that Charlie Hunnam had been cast in the role of Christian Grey. There was the expected sour grapes when fan favorites were not selected but the vast majority of those texting and tweeting madly was that he had that Christian look. Dornan would be circumspect in coming in a close second. To be sure, there was a degree of disappointment as no actor wants to lose out on a potentially career making part.

But Jamie was quick to look beyond the part to the much bigger things in life. With *The Fall* commencing production on its second season, he would not be out of work very long. He was newly married and, in a matter of months he would become a father. For now a bit of a holiday would suffice. Jamie was not one to let a career disappointment ruin his life.

However thoughts of a holiday would be short lived. Some six weeks after the announcement and a mere three weeks before *Fifty Shades of Grey* was set to begin filming, Hunnam had a change of mind and, for more reasons than the press could count, bowed out of the film. Which immediately cast the spotlight on Jamie and a handful of other frontrunners. For his part, Jamie was torn. He was not one to wish bad tidings on anyone but the departure of Hunnam had suddenly put him back in the running.

His excitement at getting a second chance was countered by the fact that his shot at the big time was coming together much quicker than he was used to. He literally had to say yes or no at that moment. "Usually with these things, people say 'take your time'," Jamie reflected of his decision making process to *Shortlist*. "But I didn't really have a huge amount of time. So you just call on the people who represent you and the people you love collectively make a decision."

Before he knew it, Jamie was on a plane to Los Angeles where he met with director Sam Taylor Johnson and, perhaps most importantly, read two scenes with his potential co-star Dakota Johnson, a condensed introductory sequence and the final scene from the book. By all accounts, Jamie did quite well in the audition and the chemistry between the two actors, as well as with the director, appeared to be quite good. Jamie saw in his possible work mates a sense of drive and professionalism very much like his own. If he got the part, he knew he would be in good stead.

But Jamie was smart enough to realize that this was a rushed situation and that they were not only looking for a good actor but a good actor right now. And while this second round of auditions had whittled down the short list, he knew he had solid competition in the still in the running Alexander Skarsgard, Billy Magnussen and Luke Bracy. Jamie was realist enough to realize, as it had been with the selection of Hunnam, it could all boil down to name recognition and, in that case, he would most certainly be trumped by Skarsgard.

Jamie clicked on the phone. On the other end of a slightly static line was director Sam Taylor Johnson. She excitedly asked Jamie how he would feel about being the object of millions of women's fantasies? At the other end of the transatlantic call, Jamie smiled, most certainly a satisfied, perhaps little boy smile.

It was all happening so quickly. There were contracts to read over and sign, arrangements for Amelia had to be made, a script that he had to familiarize himself with. But there was finally that one certainty.

Jamie was officially Christian Grey.

After the director hung up, Jamie was in a sudden state of giddiness and shock. His first instinct was to go downstairs and tell Amelia the news. But as he recalled in an *Entertainment Weekly* interview, his initial reaction was a mixture of fear and excitement for what the future would bring.

"There was a slight fear," he recalled. "But beyond everything else, I was really fucking excited."

In another time and place, Jamie would have greeted the news that would change his life with a boatload of drinks and a party like few had ever seen. But, as he related to *Today*, since this was another time and place…

…"I went downstairs where my wife was sleeping, joined her in bed and I went to sleep."

CHAPTER ONE
DAD DELIVERS BABIES

To this day, they still talk about Professor Jim Dornan's acting turn at Ireland's Bangor Grammar School. He played the lead in Lady MacBeth and, by all accounts, there was star quality in his performance.

Fortunately the gods had loftier goals for the youngster than an Oscar.

"My dad delivers babies," Jamie would tell journalist J.P. Watson some years later. "Can you imagine that?"

Jamie tossed off that comment in a bemused but easily reverent manner. There's a sincerity and deeply felt emotional bond that shines through at the mere mention of his father. They have been through a lot together, in facing real life and the world. And it is easy to see why those who have broached the subject with Jamie have often reported a wistful, sometimes close to tearful look.

That Professor James Dornan has spent a good part of his life simply delivering babies is a bit of an understatement. Over the course of more than 40 years and primarily in Northern Ireland, although his attitudes and progressive thinking have had worldwide impact, Jim Dornan has delivered more than 6000 babies, has been a pioneer in the ever-evolving science of Obstetrics and Gynecology and a quietly outspoken advocate for the life of the mother and the life in the womb.

Those latter traits being the by product of an upbringing and family attitude towards equal rights for women in all ways. "I inherited a total commitment to women and women's rights," he explained in an article that appeared in *Jamie Dornan Fans*. "We are all that way in the family (his daughters and son) and I have influenced them that way."

Jim is noted for being quiet, introspective but always on personal and professional point. Never one to rush in without the benefit of a lot of research and contemplation, but easygoing and good company in social gatherings, Jim was notorious for being a deep thinker as well as somebody who would openly embrace new ideas. Over the years he would author numerous medical papers that encouraged progressive thinking in the areas of women and medicine.

A quiet but determined physician in the tradition of television's Marcus Welby, Jim was brought into early contact with the plights of the less fortunate through his father who worked as an accountant for several organizations dealing with special needs children, adults and the underprivileged. It was at the suggestion of his father, who cited the prestige as well as the economic advantages of being a doctor, that Jim steered a life course into a career to medicine. It would remain for the occasion of Jim witnessing his first live birth in the 1970's, which he would describe in a *News Letter* conversation as "awesome" to drive him to specialize in Obstetrics and Gynecology.

Needless to say, Jamie often overflows with

Inside Grey's Anatomy: The Unauthorized Biography of Jamie Dornan

positive when the subject of his father comes up, as it did in a recent conversation with The Sunday Times. "He's an astonishing man. I find him hugely impressive in pretty much every facet of his being."

But as Jamie would jokingly admit in a conversation with *The Scotsman*, his father may well have given up one passion for another. "He became a doctor and had a very fulfilled life but I think there's a part of him that always wanted to explore acting."

To the extent that, when Jim was offered an opportunity to attend London's famed Royal Academy of Dramatic Art, he was seriously thinking of putting medicine aside in favor of the stage. But firm hands from his parents and an enormous dose of practicality would ultimately prevail. Jamie would relate years later in a *Sunday Times* conversation that his father's plans were stalled by a firm hand.

"He didn't take the opportunity to attend RADA. Back then things were different. His parents were very strict and they wanted him to be a doctor. But I think that there was a part of him that would have loved to have lived out the acting life."

And so, with any regrets seemingly put aside Jim opted for medicine and later love.

Jim had always seemed to have two simple requirements when it came to his love life, dedication and a sense of humor. Both of those requirements were definitely at the forefront when he met and married a registered nurse named Lorna. But as Jamie would recall in *Now Daily* in later years that she also had other qualities that may well have influenced her son in later years. "My mum was extremely glamorous and beautiful and into style."

The couple settled in Hollywood County Down, a stone's throw away from the center of Belfast Northern Ireland. Hollywood Country Down was a fairly peaceful place to live. It was outdoorsy and florid with a small town attitude. Many upwardly mobile professionals who did their business easily in nearby Belfast chose Hollywood Country Down as a languid and easy place to live as well as being a stone's throw away from the more cosmopolitan Belfast.

But there was always an underlying sense of tension on the horizon when it came to Belfast and Northern Ireland. Locals called it The Troubles, a decades old and seemingly never-ending strife centering on religious and political differences.

This was an adventurous time and place for the couple to be settling. Political and social upheavals between Ireland and the UK had long since risen to dangerous levels and the normally tranquil city of Hollywood was not immune from the sounds and headlines of revolution, bomb scares and the often violent clashes between Protestants and Catholics over ideologies seemingly incapable of compromise.

Jamie would often acknowledge the dichotomy of growing up in an affluent, largely peaceful community and, yet, having to watch for danger at just about every turn in a conversation with *The Telegraph*. "Growing up, it was always like 'let's go shopping in Belfast'," he recalled. "But then there would be like a bomb scare and you would go ah right fuck it. You get used to that. And then it becomes a part of your life."

And it was within these often trying times that Jim and Lorna made their home. Jim's reputation and notoriety continued to ascend in the medical community.

He would go on to chair several well known advocacy groups and his quiet yet incessant demeanor was at the forefront of many advances in Obstetrics and Gynecology. Jim would spend much of his early career advancing his career by chairing important advocacy conferences in Belfast and other areas of Europe where his quiet yet straightforward demeanor and attitude brought accolades and respect from the medical community. But the accolades usually stopped at the hospital door when he reverted to Dr. Dornan and returned to his day job of bringing life into the world.

It was also during this period that the couple, after five years of trying unsuccessfully to have children, started their family with the arrival of two daughters, Liesa and Jessica.

Jim related to *The Irish News* that, on the occasion of the birth his first child Liesa, he was less than stalwart at the time of her birth. "I was physically nauseated witnessing the pain of labor suffered by my wife and was finally put out the door. Consequently I was barred from attending the birth of my first child."

Midway through 1981, Lorna was once again pregnant with their third child. The couple had never made public a preference for their children, girl or boy, all that mattered was that they were healthy and happy. But it would be an understatement to say that the thought of having a son had not crossed Jim's mind. However at the end of the day, he was a firm believer in what the fates allow.

And unlike the birth of his first child, when Lorna went into labor with what would be their last, Jim was front and center when Lorna gave birth.

James Jamie Dornan was born on May 1, 1982.

CHAPTER TWO
SHORT, CUTE AND BLOODY

Jamie was born into a family that had a long history stepped in traditional religion. His grandparents on both his father and mother's side were Methodist lay preachers. Jim and Lorna were Protestant but, given their careers and attitudes in the medical history, were not bound to strictly traditional and conservative edicts.

Consequently Jamie and his two older sisters were raised in a hybrid environment of conservative and liberal thinking. The parent's word on any matter was ultimately the final say and most childhood rebelliousness was dealt with accordingly. But by all accounts there really was not a whole lot of rebel in Jamie to consider. From the earliest age, Jamie was a go with the flow kind of child. Whatever was happening in his world was where he was at before something else drove him on. The young Jamie was pretty much what any child of a certain age was like, which was nothing too far reaching beyond the moment.

Jamie would acknowledge in a This Is London interview that, from his earliest memories, the seeds ,a mixture of authoritative and just as often jokingly, were being planted in his head that he would most certainly follow in the family business. "My grandparents were very strict and regularly admonished any contrary thoughts with 'No, you're going to medical school!' "

However such pronouncements would ultimately not be set in stone. From his birth, Jamie was encouraged by his parents to explore his world and, even at a very young age, to express his individuality and creativity.

And along the way, Jamie would forge a very close bond with his older sisters. Jim and Lorna were not hardcore feminists but their immersion into the science of Obstetrics and Gynecology had made them supporters of women and their lives. Consequently the Dornan family concept was set up to include a very protective and supportive dynamic in which Jamie, at an early age, instinctively took on the role of protector.

By all accounts Jamie took to his world with childlike enthusiasm and developed a deep love for the place he grew up. Many years later he would acknowledge as much in an interview with journalist Mr. Porter when he said "Hollywood is where my heart is. It's where my heart is. I have no desire to leave."

However those thoughts were tempered by the fact that he was growing up in troubled times and often experienced the political and social upheaval first hand, albeit in small and passing moments. He was a child but his association with 'The Troubles' caused him to grow up quickly and in ways that would linger through the years.

Years later Jamie would acknowledge in *British Vogue* that growing up in and around Belfast in the 80's and 90's was a double-edged sword. "Belfast in the 80's was still not a great place to be but I wouldn't have changed my upbringing for the world. I went to school in Belfast, all my mates were from there. I was in a protected part of it. I'm not trying to sell it like I saw the worst of it. But we definitely saw things and there certainly was fear and tension that doesn't exist now."

Through it all there would be an element of sensitivity that would grow to be a bedrock of his growing maturity and personality. At a very young age, Jamie would tell anybody who would listen that he was going to be a forest ranger when he grew up, a career born of his love of animals.

Although Jamie grew up a fairly skinny child, and having been diagnosed with asthma at an early age he was never far from his inhaler, he was physically fit by most standards and, by age eight, he was actively pursuing the sport of golf with a reported respectable handicap for his age. By age 11, his athletic passion turned to the rough and tumble game of rugby and he was a regular participant in the various youth leagues around Belfast.

During his childhood he also became keenly aware of his family tree and, in particular, his relation to legendary actress Greer Garson. "Greer Garson was my great aunt," Jamie explained to *The Scotsman*. "She was my grandmother's first cousin. When you're a kid you're not really watching things like *Mrs. Miniver* and *Pride & Prejudice* so I wasn't really that aware of her."

Inside Grey's Anatomy: The Unauthorized Biography of Jamie Dornan

Throughout his early years, Jamie was the picture of a well-rounded Belfast lad. He was alternately outgoing and laidback, often to the point of shyness, but he made friends easily, largely through his interest in sports and in school where he was reportedly a better than average, if often reluctant student. Like most pre- teens about to enter that awkward and confusing stage, Jamie was well aware of his looks, especially as it related to his growing interest in the opposite sex. And as he would relate in Now Daily and other publications, he was not always thrilled with what he saw.

""It's not like I cleaned up with the girls," he said. "I always looked young and very small. I would get real tired of being called cute."

But he would laughingly recall in *Fabulous* that even cute eventually led him to get up close and personal with the opposite sex. "My first kiss was that classic behind the bike sheds when I was 12 or 13 years old with a girl whose name I don't remember."

By the time Jamie entered secondary school at age 14, he had pretty much made up his mind that he was destined to become a professional rugby player. But as he would recall in *Fabulous*, the guardian angel on his left shoulder had other plans. "As a teenager I started to turn in the direction of drama."

And so it was that, while maintaining good grades, the majority of his energies were devoted to his main interests, rugby and acting. Of the former he would build his body through a rather unorthodox regime of extreme physical training and fast food hamburgers. Of the later he had evolved, at a fairly young age, into a reliable character actor. So much so that barely into his teens, he was part of a youth theatrical troop that made a circuit of Northern Ireland venues, performing in such classic bits of theater as Chekov's Cherry Orchard.

But as he closed in on his 15th birthday, Jamie found himself leaning more toward sport and, particularly, rugby where he was making his athletic bones as an aggressive winger for both school and informal leagues around town.

And it was his aggressiveness, coupled with the quite expected teenage attitude, that resulted in his 'cute' face getting busted up on occasion as he recalled in *The Journal*. In one instance a tennis coach, fed up with Jamie's rebellious nature, threw a tennis ball at his face, breaking his nose. On still another occasion, a head on collision with another player on the rugby field broke his nose a second time. Admittedly painful, these literal bust ups went a long way, in Jamie's mind as well as in the coming of age world of teen macho, in giving him immediately credibility with his peers.

Jim and Lorna were well aware of what was going on with Jamie and, as they had previously done with his sisters, they, with rare exception, gave him the freedom to discover and grow.

A deep thinker even at that age, Jamie was starting to round into shape as somebody who would not tread a predictable career path. He balked at the idea of a 9:00 to 5:00 existence and thought daily train rides to a sedate and predictable life as a cog in the corporate machine was repugnant.

Jamie was thinking of a future done up his way.

CHAPTER THREE
TROUBLES

By the time Jamie turned 15, he had become quite familiar with the term 'The Troubles.' On the grand scale, where ideologies, religions and political and social views, made often bloody front page headlines and grim and granny video images on the nightly news, 'The Troubles' had long been a part of his daily sojourns into his world. It was like part of the scenery.

"I think people from Northern Ireland have some kind of unspoken general feeling," Jamie once philosophized in a conversation with *The Telegraph*. "They know what it's like to be around segregation."

But around the time of his 15th birthday, the idea of 'The Troubles' was brought home to Jamie and his family in a very personal way. Lorna was showing signs of not being well just days after Jim and she returned from a holiday in Madrid. An initial exam indicated an easily treatable jaundice. But when Lorna continued in declining health, a follow up examination found that Jamie's mother had pancreatic cancer and the pronouncement was grave. The cancer was inoperable and she had approximately 18 months to live.

That was suddenly Jamie's reality. "There's no easy time to lose a parent," Jamie reflected in *The Telegraph*. "It's a very transitional time, being that age, and a very impressionable time. It was a horrific period in my life."

But Jamie's fear and sadness were tempered by the fact that the family would have 18 months together. Taking the lead from his stoic father, Jamie and his sisters took comfort in the fact that they still had time to be with their mother.

"It was a bizarre, huge and awful point in my life," Jamie had said in several media outlets including *Now!* "The comfort was knowing that it was inoperable, knowing what the outcome would be, rather than clinging onto some kind of hope that she was going to be with us."

The family was literally on hold during the coming months, essentially sleepwalking through their daily lives and taking every opportunity to be with their mother. Jamie was particularly torn, putting on a stolid face as he worked through his studies and final exams. When he was with his mother he watched, often torn, as Lorna, seemingly on the fence when it came to religion, had suddenly turned to faith in her final days.

"I struggle with the whole religion thing myself," Jamie acknowledged to *Now!*. "But my mother found faith when she was dying and I totally respected that."

For his part, Jamie's father would acknowledge in *Irish Central* that he gained even more respect for his son during those dark days. "You know everything about Jamie has made me proud. The way he responded to his mother's illness and death, he is an incredibly level headed, solid guy."

Jamie's mother succumbed to her illness midway through 1998. The young boy took it particularly hard, recalling on more than one occasion that his mother's death permanently shaped his attitudes about mortality and death. As the family struggled to put their lives back together, Jamie seemed to be particularly in need of a change of scenery. With his father and he in agreement, Jamie would now be boarded at Methodist College Belfast.

In looking back on the decision, Jamie came across as not totally on board with living at the school in a conversation with *Out*. "We felt it would be better for me. I guess." But for whatever hesitancy the youngster may have felt about his living away from home so soon after his mother's death, he ultimately would go along with the decision.

Given the recent turmoil, Jamie appeared to thrive in this new life situation according to the school's vice principal Norma Gallagher in a conversation with *Radio Times*.

"He was very modest," she recalled. "One of his best subjects was drama. I remember him making a very good milkman in Blood Brothers and Baby Face in Bugsy Malone."

While at Methodist, he also continued to flex his sporting muscles when he hooked up with the local rugby club, The Belfast Harlequins. The club had a sterling reputation in Ireland as one of the premiere rugby youth groups and had long had a reputation for turning out players ready for the professional ranks. By this time Jamie's body had fleshed out into a well-muscled body, one capable of lightning strikes on the pitch. Jamie's success in the youth ranks once again had the youngster thinking in terms of a professional sports career.

Jamie was considered far from an academic during his time at Methodist. But he was one who could buckle down and do what had to be done, hence his ability to pass three very cerebral levels, Classics, English Literature and History of Art. With an emphasis on 'just barely'.

While at Methodist, Jamie made the acquaintance of fellow classmate David Alexander. The pair had much in common. They had the same temperament and interests and could literally talk for hours on any number of subjects. But perhaps more telling was the fact that David had lost his father when he was not much older than Jamie. They became fast friends. And along the way, the seeds of a future together in music were laid.

"We shared some of the same musical interests," Jamie told *The Sunday Times*. "At one point we recorded some stuff back in Ireland, purely to have something on CD. Now and then we would rehearse a bit but we weren't taking it too seriously."

Jamie was seemingly content and comfortable in this educational environment and realistic with dealing with the death of his mother and moving on with his life. When one year and two weeks after his mother died, tragedy once again struck.

Four of Jamie's friends from Methodist were driving down a road when they were involved in a horrendous crash. All of Jamie's mates, as well as a nine year old boy, perished in the crash. Jamie was totally devastated when he heard the news.

"It was a totally hideous, life changing

circumstance that you carry every day," he recalled to *The Telegraph*. "And that's not going to change. These are events that form your identity and probably not in a positive way. I think it [the crash] definitely changed my view of mortality and death."

But, as he recalled in an *Irish Mirror* conversation, the twin tragedies left him with some deeper issues and scars. "When my mum died, I was angry at the start and I still get angry sometimes. My mum's death made me more accepting of things but the enormity of it all still hits me in waves."

Jamie became withdrawn and quiet in the wake of this second tragedy. His father sensed the adverse reaction in his son and strongly suggested that Jamie get therapy. To what degree the therapy helped is open to conjecture but as Jamie offered in several media interviews including one with *The Sun*, he seemed resigned to the reality and his ability to cope with his losses of first his mother and then his friends.

"Therapy got me through it. I'm not sure how I would have coped without it. It's awful to say but it's almost better that it happened early on because it prepared me for situations that might arise in later life."

Jamie's father, Jim, was on board with his son's sentiments and acknowledged in *The Belfast Telegraph* that, in its own way, molded Jamie's attitude toward life. "Obviously his life has been colored by the death of his mother and his friends. I think it has left him with a great sense of comradeship and all of it had made him very thoughtful about his life in general and what he wants to do."

That he emerged from therapy with a realistic

attitude toward his twin tragedies would seem a successful transition. But in the same *The Sun* interview Jamie dropped a notion that might have caused

more than one observer to speculate how these deaths had truly turned him to emotional stone.

"It's just some shit that happened."

CHAPTER FOUR
MODEL CITIZEN

Jamie was literally and emotionally adrift when he graduated from Methodist in late 1999. Academically, the pressures of the recent tragedies in his life, had reduced his interest in school rather dramatically. He had literally sleepwalked through his final year with, at best, average grades.

Although therapy had helped somewhat in dealing with the tragedies of the past year, the feelings of loss were never far from his thoughts. And in his shaky emotional state, he would acknowledge that he had his dreams but no concrete plans for the future. The dreams, quite simply, were rugby and acting. But the reality was that he needed a "real job" to pay the rent in the meantime.

His disinterest in pursuing anything other than a paycheck resulted in a series of uninteresting jobs that did not last very long. High up on what he considered the most "hideous" of the dead end jobs was working for a call center that sold gas and electricity and driving cars around at an auction house. Of these ventures, Jamie related to *The Times* "It [the selling job] only lasted a week. The car driving job, I only lasted a day on that."

Jamie's father was surprisingly tolerant and patient with his son's inability to hold a job and his seeming aimlessness, allowing that the loss of his mother and friends should allow him some time to find himself.

Which was why, when he matriculated to Teesside University in North Eastern UK, Jamie was apparently off in another life direction as he set himself up as a less than enthusiastic marketing major. Jamie remained a largely solitary soul and did not stand out to any great degree, especially when it came to the ladies.

"I was very shy," he related to *The Belfast Telegraph*. "I'm not going to say that was the only reason that I didn't do well with them but I just didn't."

Jamie's goals for higher education quickly ran afoul of boredom and the quick onset of disinterest. By his own estimation, as reported in *The Times*, he attended a total of nine hours of lectures during that first year with a blank expression on this face. "I didn't have an idea what they were talking about." But most likely to appease his father, he kept at it but just barely.

Jamie was literally going through the motions of trying to ultimately land a 'respectable' job. And as he offered in *Shortlist Mode*, he was slowly but surely losing his grip on all things practical. "I knew I was not the type of person who would sit down and type numbers all day. My brain just didn't work that way. I never thought I would end up sitting in an office."

What he would do when not in lecture halls was spend his time playing rugby and drinking beer. And his party life did not only stop at the UK border. Even years later, Jamie related in a *Daily Record* conversation that across the border in Scotland was also a stop for aimlessness and high jinks. "I've done my time in Scotland. I spent a lot of time there with student friends. They were all in Glasgow and so we'd spend many a fun night there. We'd go to places like The Garage and The Student Union. I doubt I was a hit with the Scottish ladies."

Of even more concern in Jamie's (as well as his sister's) life was the fact that, less than a year after his mother's death, Jim had fallen in love with a young Pakistan obstetrics trainee named Samina. It was almost an afterthought that Samina was 20 years younger than their father and of a different faith (Muslim). For Jamie and his sisters it did not come as a surprise that their father was in another relationship so soon after their mother's death. It had been a topic of conversation throughout their parent's relationship that if one parent died before the other, the surviving parent would most certainly move on with their life and into another relationship.

Jim acknowledged in *The Belfast Telegraph* that being aware of their parents' wishes did not necessarily make for a smooth acceptance. "My kids have been great, though no one would say that it was easy at the start. They knew it was going to happen, they just did not know when it would happen and who it would be."

However by the time Jim and Samina married in 2002, his grown children had become attached to their stepmother in different ways as he explained in *The Belfast Telegraph*. "Samina is more of a friend to the girls. With Jamie it was more of a maternal role."

Jim's remarks immediately opened up a whole new can of speculation. For all of his perceived individuality and male oriented attitudes, Jamie had always had the kind of family interaction that was largely feminine. With his sister's being older and already on with their own lives, the death of Jamie's mother had most likely left him without that all important female anchor.

Liesa and Jesse had inevitably moved on in their personal and professional lives, leaving Jamie largely alone in his thoughts and frustrations. He had known that marketing had been a halfhearted backup to the passions that continued to drive him. He continued to make strides with the Belfast Harlequins and the consensus of those who watched him was that he had a reasonable shot of making it as a rugby professional. But in the back of Jamie's mind, there was the specter of life as an actor that continued to dog him.

Jamie dropped out of Teesside after his first year and concentrated primarily on gathering up a pro rugby deal. He became a gypsy, playing a lot of rugby for little or no money. It just was not happening in the timely manner that Jamie had hoped for but, short of rugby, he had no idea of what his next step would be.

That's when his sister Liesa threw Jamie a lifeline.

Model Behavior was the latest in a seemingly never-ending cycle of reality/talent shows. In *Model Behavior* a group of wannabe models live together and perform different challenges on route to a first prize of a modeling contract and a clear shot to fame and fortune. The show had been running commercials and ads seeking contestants for the show and Liesa, perhaps more as a lark than anything else, suggested that her brother might want to take a shot.

Initially Jamie brushed off the idea, his inherent manliness telling him that modeling was far from a true man's occupation. But when a friend offered to go along with him to an audition, he agreed, expecting nothing to come of it except a day of goofing off in London. Long story short, Jamie's friend washed out. Jamie was selected for the show.

In a *British Vogue* interview, Jamie laughingly recalled that his tenure on *Model Behavior* was brief. "I think I made it to day two before they said 'okay, that's enough, see ya'," Jamie, to that point, had been a fairly cool head when it came to dealing with rejection and disappointment. But, initially, this washout at the hands of what he perceived as a tacky talent show hit him hard. "I was gutted," he told *ASOS* of that rejection. "But I thought 'fuck it!' "

But Jamie had been seen enough in those two days that, upon his dismissal from the show, he was immediately inundated by offers from agencies and photographers. Jamie went home to Belfast to contemplate this sudden turn and what he should do about it.

He was still not thrilled with the notion of becoming what he considered the empty-headed male model stereotype. But he did concede that modeling might give him a chance to network in the world of acting which was now, in his own mind, turning into his ultimate goal. It finally boiled down to the encouragement of Samina, who like his father had sensed the aimlessness in Jamie, to encourage her stepson to go to London and give modeling a try.

Liesa, already a London resident, had offered her brother a place to stay while he got his bearings. His only other alternative, rugby, had not panned out the way Jamie had hoped.

Finally in 2002 Jamie, on nothing more than a wing and a prayer and a handful of business cards, left Belfast bound for London and the big city lights. Jamie's intent was to meet with drama schools. But Jamie was the first to acknowledge in *This Is London* and *The Evening Standard* that the first six months were far from his finest hour.

"I drank too much and didn't get my act together," he said. "I worked in a pub for six months and then I would end up crying every night."

And the main reason for the tears was that, after a short stay with his sister, Jamie proved his independence by insisting on moving out on his own and into a squalid flat in Hackney, East London where his pub wages barely provided the rent, let alone what he considered the necessities of life.

"Despite the fact that the flat was so cheap, I felt like I couldn't afford a kettle," he revealed in an interview with *The Stage*. "To make tea I'd leave the hot water running until it got scolding."

One day Jamie's father came into town for a visit. They decided to watch a rugby match on television and, in Jamie's case, that meant attempting to make heads and tails of the match while watching Jamie's ancient black and white television which featured a constantly rolling picture.

"The picture kept flickering as I sat with my dad, with a cup of tea I had made from a hot water tap, watching this pathetic excuse for a telly" he recalled to

The Stage. "Finally my dad just looked at me and said, 'Son, you can't live like this.' He put his foot down and helped me get out of that situation."

This was a tense moment between father and son. Jamie had made the move to London largely to show his father that he could be independent. He balked at the idea of his father stepping in to set things right. But he knew in his gut that living in a tumble down apartment in a bad part of town was not helping his mental state and so he did not put up much of a fight.

Through some acquaintances made during his stint on *Model Behavior*, Jamie continued to play rugby on a purely informal basis. The meetings with drama schools did not materialize and eventually Jamie decided to give modeling his full attention. And those first baby steps would prove the most humbling. As described by *The New York Times*, many was the day that Jamie wandered in and out of runway model casting sessions, considered by many in the fashion business as the lowest possible run on the ladder but, for the newcomer, a way to make some money and possibly get some exposure. Be it his inexperience or his look, Jamie painfully recalled, years later, that he would never get hired.

It was about that time that Select Modeling, one of the more prestigious modeling agencies in the UK, and the agency that had offered a modeling contract to the winner of *Model Behavior*, signed Jamie to a contract. Select had the reputation of positioning its clients for high profile, and lucrative, ad campaigns and photo shoots. They were, like their name suggested, particular in who they took on. Their requirements were simple. The look was everything.

And although it did not dawn on Jamie at that point that he was physically striking in a model sort of way, Jamie quite simply had the look.

Jamie quickly discovered two aspects of the modeling business that he liked. To his way of thinking, it was relatively easy work. And it paid quite well.

CHAPTER FIVE
DORNAN GOES KNIGHTLEY

Jamie's earliest modeling assignments were nothing to write home about. His youthful, alternately expressive and brooding good looks, had made him a natural for the pre-teen catalogue market. Consequently his most notorious work, in the likes of Abercrombie & Fitch and similar catalogues, was more posed and often cheesy looking rather than sensual.

Jamie must have had a good laugh at the idea of projecting innocent smiles and good natured poses required of those shoots that saw him racing back and forth to change clothes and return to the set. In Jamie's eyes this first step in the modeling industry was not to be taken seriously. But he could not argue with the fact that it was paying the bills.

When not modeling, Jamie was continuing his rugby activities, as well as the occasional round of clay pigeon shooting, which as he explained in his *British Vogue* interview, he was doing his best to keep the inevitable injuries from his modeling agency who would be less than thrilled if injuries marred his marketable face and body. "It got to the point where I didn't tell my agent that I was playing rugby."

Mentally and emotionally Jamie, from the outset, did not seem to fit the male model role. He was relaxed, willing to do what was expected and then move on. There was no sense of frantic conforming to the clichés of body type, the drive to quickly move up the modeling ladder and, while always professional, there was no sense of competitiveness in his day to day interaction with other models. Those attitudes alone, according to fashion observers made Jamie a bit of an oddity, somebody who had the potential to step out from the pack.

While he was struggling, Jamie, often unbeknownst to him, was making a major impression on an all-important segment of the modeling and fashion industry, the gay community. The likes of photographers and fashion designers Bruce Weber, Carter Smith, Steven Miesel and Hedi Slimane. Weber, in particular are given credit in most chronologies as the ones who kickstarted Jamie's modeling career with early work that brought him to the attention of fashion professionals and tastemakers.

"I certainly did not know much about fashion years ago," he told *The Scotsma*n, "but I knew who Bruce Weber was. We got on well and so for the first couple of years I pretty much only worked with him."

But while Jamie was paying the rent, the top flight assignments modeling for major companies seemed to be eluding him. That's when his modeling agency had the inspired idea of doing a formal meet and greet for their client in America. His looks, attitude and that tantalizing Irish accent were an immediate hit with the US fashion industry and it was not long before offers from across the pond were pouring in.

Jamie's big fashion breaks came in 2002 when his growing word of mouth resulted in specifically designed editorial spreads in the magazines *GQ* and *Attitudes*. Jamie brought a sense of natural and laidback to the photo sessions. It was a style that many models could have easily imitated but Jamie made it his own in a matter of fact, at ease manner. Jim Moore, the veteran creative director at *GQ*, told *The New York Times* that Jamie was immediately something special.

"In a span of 20 years I've seen maybe four models who have what Jamie Dornan has. And what is that? For a start there's the way he photographs. He is the male Kate Moss."

Moore went on to quantify the look Jamie has. His proportions are slightly off. He has a slight build, he's on the small side by model standards but his lean frame makes him look taller. "And he's relaxed. He's a model by not modeling."

Within the year there was a definite buzz growing up around Jamie in the modeling and fashion world. But for the 20 year old, it was still an everyday hustle of auditions and callbacks. And despite stories depicting Jamie as an instant success, the reality was that in 2002 and for some time after, he was just one of a seemingly endless crowd vying for the attention of designers and photographers. He would often chuckle at the irony of going off to a shoot in Paris and then coming back to London for more failure. Fortunately he was being paid quite handsomely when he did work and so he would not be waiting anxiously by the phone. And it was not like he was idle.

The pipedream of musical stardom with his school chum David was still being addressed on a regular basis. They had decided to call themselves Sons of Jim in difference to the fact that both of their fathers were named Jim. They had also begun experimenting with a slightly more pop friendly sound akin to the band Counting Crows. Keen observers in the band's formative woodshedding indicated that Jamie was possessed of a better than average singing voice and a quietly determined performing stance. Sons of Jim were pop enough to be radio friendly but presented a more mature counter to the reigning teeny bop sound. Sons of Jim showed promise.

Jamie continued plugging away as a model, working occasionally and, along the way, gathering good word of mouth about his look and, perhaps more importantly, his professionalism. But, in his private moments, Jamie, who presented a stolid man's man persona to the world, was already dreading almost every aspect of his chosen profession and, even more glaringly, his fellow models.

"I only did the Milan Fashion Week once and it was fucking horrible," he candidly recalled in *Mode Magazine*. "What guy would enjoy that? Hanging out with a bunch of fucking douche models, each one of them saying 'ah, I saw you in that campaign, really good stuff'. I was like fuck off! I didn't want to talk about what the job was like."

Resentment aside, the bottom line was that Jamie was very good at what he was doing and the result was that, in 2003, the reluctant model received what many look back on as 'his big break' when he was selected to be one half of the modeling attraction in a photo shoot for established jewelers Asprey London opposite actress Keira Knightley.

Keira had come to prominence with a mixture of small independent films and commercial blockbusters that included *Star Wars Episode 1: The Phantom Menace, Bend It Like Beckham* and *Pirates of The Caribbean: The Curse of The Black Pearl* and was well on her way to a career that would feature the actress in both mainstream studio films and the period dramas that would become her specialty. It went without saying that Keira had it all over Jamie in terms of being established.

And while Jamie, in his limited contact with the press to that point, had been quiet, shy and self-deprecating, Keira had long had a reputation for being very open and, occasionally, a bit outrageous when it came to the media. To the extent that the recent end of her relationship with actor Del Synott had been very public and above board.

Jamie was intent on the job at hand when he flew to Manhattan for the Asprey shoot. He knew Keira by reputation and hoped the on screen chemistry would be there. It was the proverbial icing on the cake when the two models immediately hit it off. They were casual and easy in conversation and, for the camera's eye, the appeared an ideal mix of looks and body types.

The results of the Asprey shoot showcased an interesting array of attitudes, equal parts innocence and smoldering tension with an element of defiance mixed in. Playing off somebody with real acting experience forced Jamie to stretch as a model and, for the immediate future, the Asprey shoot would serve as a solid calling card for future employers.

But beyond the shoot, Jamie and Keira also struck

some emotional sparks. For Jamie first love and his first real relationship was a big step that he was somewhat hesitant at taking. But he would ultimately succumb to Keira's beauty and personality. And like his father had been with his mother, Keira presented a sly, light sense of humor that truly appealed to him. Not long after they met, Jamie and Keira were officially a couple.

It would be a relationship that would put Jamie in the public eye in a way he was not used to and that would immediately test his resolve.

Jamie had a sense of how show business relationships usually played out and he felt early on that one of the biggest potential problems could most certainly be avoided, the difference in their respective celebrity status. On that account, as he told *ES Magaz*ine back in the day, he had no illusions of grandeur. "I don't think I'm every going to be as famous as her."

Nor was he completely surprised when a night out on the town, something usually low key and barely acknowledged in Jamie's circle, had, with Keira, turned into a literal three ring circus of media attention in which paparazzi seemed always in their face, snapping away. Keira seemed fine with the attention and Jamie, to his credit, got used to the idea that his comings and goings were now regularly plastered on the covers of the tabloids and gossip magazines.

Jamie's patience would often be tested during his relationship with Keira. With their respective celebrity status, a lot of nights out would regularly center around industry events, film and fashion premieres and parties. Jamie would tell The Times in the coming years that it was all becoming boring and fairly quickly. "Why am I here?," he groused. "It's not fun at all. Too much champagne and I hate champagne."

But Jamie knew that being seen at all the right parties and being in the paparazzi maelstrom was part of the process.

"Initially I was indifferent to it," he told *This Is London*. "It was just something that happens to a couple in that position. It didn't affect me in a massive way."

But there were media members who soon floated the notion that Jamie was benefitting by his relationship with Keira by having his celebrity public profile rising. Jamie, perhaps with a bit of ego and frustration simmering below the surface, denied to *This Is London* that being with Keira was helping his career. "Certainly from a professional standpoint, I don't think it has affected anything that has to do with anything."

Coming out of most male model's mouths, the notion of not taking anything too seriously would seem to be just Model Speak 101. But Jamie was often quite quotable in his nonchalance. And, most importantly, believable.

"I just don't take anything too seriously," he told *The New York Times*. And going into late 2003, who was to argue. Because not taking anything too seriously had put Jamie on the road to a fine career.

If Jamie only knew it.

CHAPTER SIX
JAMIE'S CALVINS

Clothing, fragrance and makeup giant Calvin Klein was one of the hottest brands on the planet To reach the level of brand was no small feat. You had to be smart, calculating and an out of the box thinker. Calvin Klein was most certainly that.

Decidedly hip and uber trendy, the company made its bones in the world of fashion, marketing and advertising and, in that arena, the company was nothing if not daring and always controversial. A 1995 ad campaign for Calvin Klein Jeans was roundly criticized for being kiddie porn. And a true adherent of the adage that 'sex sells', Calvin Klein models are almost universally young with perfect bodies and looks and the ideal tools for suggestive posing.

When it was announced that Jamie had been selected, along with model Natalia Vodianova for the latest round of advertising for Calvin Klein Jeans, the word in the fashion world was that these ads would most certainly be the most suggestive and boundary pushing in the history of the company. Rather than be concerned, Jamie was thrilled at the opportunity of an A-list job. Calvin Klein was a definite step up out of

Inside Grey's Anatomy: The Unauthorized Biography of Jamie Dornan

the modeling pack and, to his way of thinking, Jamie was confident he could handle what was to come as he prepared himself for the shoot.

He had always been an athletic type and, when coupled with his near manic regime of daily physical workouts, there was no doubt that he was in Calvin Klein shape. It had never been much of an exaggeration when those who knew him often related that Jamie could be sitting still and still be working out.

Jamie was not too surprised when he stepped on the set of the shoot. The scenes shot, and ultimately printed in a stark mixture of blacks, whites and shadowy greys, were suggestive in the extreme and involved Jamie and his female counterpart cavorting in provocative and often suggestive positions and angles and glistening through various combinations of oil and water. While the purpose was to highlight the jeans, the result was rather a highly charged series of erotic art moments. And the erotic moments were not lost on Jamie

"Yes that was my bum," he jokingly reflected in *Glamour Chick*. He would later acknowledge his various states of undress in that shoot with a quote from *Jamie Dornan News* of that shoot "I hope that's the closest I'll ever come to porn."

But, as Jamie would discover in this and future Calvin Klein shoots, life in Calvin Klein's world was a dizzying array of photographers who showcased creative artistic instincts and allowed him to do the same. "They're good at just letting me be me," he told *Hello Magazine*. "and not just turning me into something else. I didn't have to change."

And what was required of him in that first Calvin Klein campaign, photographed by Mikael Jansson, was a slightly different, albeit twisted take on sexuality. In many of the pictures, Jamie, all glistening and in super tight jeans, is seen as the submissive, often being literally and figuratively ravished by Naltalia as the sexual huntress/aggressor. The concept and the conceit of it all allowed Jamie to dig deeper than a model normally has to, displaying the feminine side of dominance and submission in a totally masculine body.

What Jamie had not completely prepared himself for was the fact that, as part of a massive marketing campaign for Calvin Klein Jeans that year, a massive billboard was about to go up on Houston Street in New York that would catapult the young model literally into the world spotlight.

And with not a whole lot on.

Jamie, in conversation with *ASOS*, recalled the day he arrived at Houston Street location in time to see the monster billboard of the ad being unveiled. "There was a huge poster of Natalia Vodinova biting my arse on Houston Street in New York. I stood there in morbid fascination as they draped the next piece of the puzzle down."

The billboard was a classic by Calvin Klein standards, Jamie on his stomach while Natalia, having pulled his jeans down to reveal his naked buttocks, is literally chewing on his naked bottom while seemingly in the midst of mindless passion. Most who saw the image, looking up from the sidewalk or from their cars as they drove past, were amazed, many were shocked at the explicitness of it all. And consequently a whole lot of people with tighter moral values bombarded city officials with demands that the billboard be taken down. Eventually it was but, in an item that appeared *in Jamie Dornan News*, the model defended the image.

"Calvin Klein wants to be controversial. So if people are demonstrating under a billboard of me getting my arse bitten by Natalia, then that's a win for them."

The Calvin Klein shoot would also tag Jamie with a nickname, The Golden Torso. It was a title that would haunt him for years and would range in his mind from amusement to embarrassment. But for better or worse he was now The Golden Torso. But in the fashion world The Golden Torso became synonymous with a look and a style that ad agencies were salivating to produce and so throughout much of 2004, Jamie was literally hopscotching from one gig to another, pulling in major money and cultivating a seemingly new level of sex and eroticism for the next wave of fashion.

Through the remainder of 2004, Keira and Jamie continued to find the time to be together. But it was not always easy. Two separate careers that often took them to different parts of the world was the most obvious challenge the couple faced. Finding time to be alone was a whole other matter.

Jamie's appearance in the Calvin Klein ads had suddenly catapulted him into that pop culture grey area in which models can truly be rock stars. Factor in Keira's continued rise in Hollywood and it was not surprising that, everywhere the couple went, the movie premieres, prestigious film festivals and the expected fashion week appearances, they were on the paparazzi's hit list. As the relationship nurtured, Jamie began to have less patience with the constant intrusion.

"Everybody has a different opinion about living in the public eye," he told *Variety*. "In a good way it made me more resilient and a lot stronger." But that even handedness on the subject had all but gone out the window by the end of 2004 and was replaced by no small degree of resentment.

"It's a strange environment to find yourself in," he groused to *The London Evening Standard*. "being hounded and followed. It's really hideous. Fucking hell! The paparazzi are cretins. That's making a choice to be a perverted fuckhead."

But there was more going on for Jamie in his relationship with Keira than joining the chorus of universal hate for the paparazzi. It was much deeper than that. This was Jamie's first serious relationship and he was raised in a traditional world where men took the lead in relationships and life. Consequently, he was instinctively protective of Keira, as witness his closeness to her in endless pictures and, no, not in a 'we're together and we're in love' pose. There was something manly and protective in his look and stance for those who looked deeper than the superficial.

And so it was in a conversation with *The Daily Telegraph* that Jamie was decidedly protective as he talked about his relationship with Keira. "Dating Keira showed how rotten the whole thing can be. A young girl is being followed around the street. There's nothing positive to say about that."

But at the end of the day, Jamie's ego and pride were on the line when it came to his relationship with Keira and he was quite candid in conversation with

The Daily Telegraph in saying that his ego and pride were taking a beating.

"The man is meant to be the alpha in the relationship on the money and power front. And clearly I was not."

But whether he was personally demeaned or not, Jamie was definitely in demand and a top dog professionally. Throughout the early months of 2005 Jamie's striking body and brooding features had him before the lens for an ad campaign for Armani Exchange, an editorial layout for *GQ* and, perhaps most significantly, the first of three contracted ad campaigns with Dior.

As befitting the high end of fashion and modeling, the Dior job was not automatic. Much like his short-lived stint on the reality series *Model Behavior*, Jamie had to endure a grueling and intense interview and elimination process as he recalled in a *New York Times* fashion piece.

"They kept eliminating people until it was down to two. I wasn't really focused on it [the audition] at the time and even at this point I question why I am the face of Dior. I don't really know why Hedi chose me. I'm not the best looking guy around."

The Dior ad played on the notion of the earlier Calvin Klein ad, upfront sexuality and temptation as displayed by a real person rather than an often skinny and, by modeling standards, cipher of male models. It also did not hurt Jamie's standing that having a natural sense of realism and, by subtle degrees, anonymity made him the ideal image for splashy magazine layouts as well as billboards and the sides of buses.

Jamie's Dior ad, as well as his previous work with

Calvin Klein, had suddenly catapulted him into the modeling major leagues. It went without saying that his day rate had gone through the proverbial roof. The ads, in various manifestations, were staying around much longer and so there was now a steady stream of residuals coming his way. With this first blush of financial security, Jamie, his traditional conservative upbringing much in evidence, passed on the normal glitzy toys that many with new money get, and instead bought a house and an apartment in London.

In the meantime his relationship with Keira was continuing. They were quite happy when spotted out together and the tabloids and gossip magazines were once again having a field day with speculations that the pair might well be on the road to marriage.

Keira, in comments that appeared in *The Chicago Tribune, People* and several other outlets, laughed off the rumors. "I'm way too young. One day in the future, maybe. But marriage and kids are not on my mind at the moment."

Through it all, Jamie would be the first to admit that there was much love and support between Keira and himself. Keira was aware of the fact that, despite having risen to become one of the most in demand models on the fashion circuit and, reportedly at his peak was making as much as ten thousand dollars a day, Jamie was constantly looking to an acting career as his ultimate goal.

"I have no intent on being a model," he told *Glamour Chick* at the time. "I don't consider myself a model in any way. I always wanted to be an actor and suddenly this [modeling] happens. Acting is still very much my focus."

Inside Grey's Anatomy: The Unauthorized Biography of Jamie Dornan

Keira took her lover at his word and offered to introduce Jamie to her agent. In what many speculated was a move to appease a top client, her agent met with Jamie. The meeting, reportedly, went well, with Jamie presenting himself as a personable young man who seemed to have the look of a 70's style leading man, much like the European old school heartthrob Jean Belmondo. The agency was well aware that there was that checkered history of models wanting to be actors to contend with and so, they cautiously agreed to take him on as a client and to get his feet wet by sending him out on a few auditions. Auditions that Jamie, drawing from his modeling experience, was quick to point out had never been a strong point.

"I'm not very good at auditions," he was quoted as saying to *Yahoo Movies* and several other outlets. "I just don't sell myself well."

It's flip and somewhat pretentious like that which had pegged Jamie, in many quarters, as lazy and unmotivated. However Jamie, in a *Bang Showbiz* interview, countered that accusation with a spirited and straightforward defense. "I was always quite a reluctant model, to my agent's never ending annoyance. I was never hugely keen on it [modeling] or doing it. It wasn't this all-consuming thing with me."

But Jamie has remained forever the mercenary pragmatist when he is on the receiving end of the inevitable question of why he does something he has no real passion for. "It would take a very foolish man to turn down the stuff that was offered to me," he told *The London Evening Standard*. You're in your twenties and people are going to give you a silly

49

amount of money to lean against a wall with your head down. Fuck me! You've got to do it."

If there was a drawback to modeling for Jamie, it was that he would constantly become the butt of good natured ribbing from his group of manly man types, long- time friends who populated his inner circle. "I would get the shit ripped out of me constantly," he told *ASOS*. "One time I did a campaign and was pulling a camp, vulnerable pose and my mates fell on the floor laughing."

By July the rumors and speculation surrounding Keira and Jamie had persisted with both *The Chicago Tribune* and *People* reporting that Jamie had actually moved into Keira's London flat. The more speculative elements of the gossip press, complete with their always in the know 'unnamed sources' were quick to paint a picture of the relationship in turmoil. To wit: How a tearful Kiera thought what Jamie and she had was truly love. How they were frantically in discussion on a daily basis on what they could do to save their relationship. And finally when they made the tearful decision to call it a day.

That was the tabloid version. By late summer, the world had the reality.

The couple officially called it quits in August, the seeming epitaph on the relationship came through Dornan's representative whose rather terse statement read "Keira and Jamie have decided to call a halt to their relationship in its current state but they remain completely committed to each other as friends."

The statement was right out of the Hollywood public relations handbook. It was vague, rather cold and seemed to satisfy nobody. The media were soon alive with speculation that it was the time apart as well as the fact that Keira's career was suddenly exploding that fed into Jamie's insecurities. For a time the tabloid and gossip press had a field day portraying Jamie as the scorned lover.

Jamie was reportedly heartbroken by the disillusion of the relationship and, sometime later, would be extremely candid in laying out his reasoning behind the breakup in conversation with WENN.

"There is a big pressure when you go out with somebody like Keira," he said. "You can feel a bit second rate and that's what started to happen. Keira could see what I was going through. She was the one who finally said, 'Okay. That's it. I've had enough.'"

CHAPTER SEVEN
POP GOES JAMIE

In the wake of his breakup with Keira, which would become official by tabloid standards in December, 2005 Jamie began to adjust to the idea that, after two years, he was once again free and single. He was spending more time with friends and was regularly seen out and about on the London club scene and roughing it up on the rugby pitch.

And with some time to kill in between modeling assignments, Jamie and his old friend David Alexander took the opportunity to rekindle their pop music career. While Jamie had found fame and fortune in London, David had been quietly pursuing a career in law. And now that he was finished with his formal education, the pair agreed it was time to give music another go.

"It wasn't a conscious decision," Jamie explained in a *Celebrities Worldwide* story. "It was an organic process. We were friends and it developed naturally."

Returning to music was a literal escape for David who ,during informal writing and recording sessions, would slip off to complete the final examinations for his law degree. The time apart had not dimmed the creative chemistry when it came to writing. There was an innate sense between the two of what worked and what did not work in writing lyrics.

David reflected on their creative relationship in an interview with *The Sunday Times*. "The two of us have come up on the same street. We can talk about it to each other. We know what the other is getting at when certain emotions are put down in song."

Those early sessions produced a handful of new songs as well as the slight reworking of their early demo material. In the spirit of DIY, the duo decided to put what they considered their most commercial song, *Fairytale*, up on a couple of iTunes style platforms to gauge a response to their music. They also took the step of venturing out into live performing as Sons of Jim with sporadic shows in Ireland and London. In London acoustic clubs like The Bedford and The Colden Club they proved a solid duo onstage with Jamie, in particular, showcasing a lilting and emotional pop vocal range.

By all accounts their shows were fairly well attended and the audiences were enthusiastic and supportive. But in a conversation with *Elle*, Jamie painted a much different picture. "I should be writing a thousand apology letters to the friends and family I dragged to our gigs over the years. Often they were the only people in the room."

What had been to that point fun and games suddenly became a bit more serious when a management firm, who had gotten wind of Sons of Jim's demo, the relative success of the song *Fairytale* and the positive reviews of their live shows and stepped in with an eye toward making Jamie and David genuine pop stars.

The first step in that direction took place when Sons of Jim were booked as the opening act for veteran Scottish singer-songwriter K.T. Tunstall on a six date UK tour. It was a new experience for Jamie and David, playing in front of larger crowds in venues like The Cockpit and Fibbers. Sons of Jim held their own in what is traditionally the opening act for a popular headliner and were the recipient of some decent reviews.

Jamie recalled the tour fondly in an interview with *The Scotsman*. "It was brilliant fun. She [Tunstall] was incredible. Watching her do what she does every night was a real treat. She was completely lovely as well."

Suddenly music was morphing into serious business. Top UK producer Brian Higgins invited the duo to his Xenomania Studios to lay down some tracks. David and Jamie soon found themselves involved with several topflight producer/writers that included Tim Kellett, Cliff Jones, Ali Thomson and Pete Glenister. By December 2005, Jamie's still lingering feelings for Keira were replaced by a seemingly endless round of professional possibilities.

Jamie would often speculate about how David and he, two rank amateurs who had started doing music as a lark, had suddenly become pop stars on the rise. Being the new name and the next big thing had its upside as they continued their musical travels in the spirit of fun. But the realist as well as the puritan in Jamie, as he recalled in *Shortlist Mode*, knew they were being led down the proverbial garden path even in the earliest days.

"We weren't really any good. We were easily

manipulated and easily led. We were ending up singing songs that we really didn't want to sing."

And Jamie's day job would often put a halt to any musical aspirations.

In fact his growing status as a top model would often have him having to put a halt to Sons of Jim to go off and do an ad campaign during much of 2005 with such now familiar suitors as Armani, Dior and GQ. Modeling wise Jamie was at ease with it all. The campaigns had seemingly all been designed to accommodate his stark personality and imagery. It was still an enjoyable and relatively easy process and the pay remained first rate. But more than ever, Jamie had music on his mind and the continued notion that somewhere down the road, acting was waiting.

Jamie and David were now preoccupied with the music, acting like little kids in a candy store amid the attention of many top producers, the nuts and bolts of sitting down with a songwriter and knocking out a potential top 40 hit. But amid the endless hours in the studio, the rehearsals and the occasional gigs, they also found time to honor their past. When things got serious enough that they felt they should create their own record label for future releases, they settled on Doorstep Records in honor of their favorite sandwich shop back in Belfast.

Sofia Coppola had been the latest member of the legendary filmmaking family to enter the family business. Going from actress to screenwriter and finally to director, making her independent film bones on the films *Virgin Suicides* and *Lost In Translation*. For her third directorial effort, *Marie Antoinette*, she was attempting a historical/pop biopic of the 18th century queen. Sofia was going for a more stylized effort and more modern telling with *Marie Antoinette* and so was populating the film with name actors. For the title role, she made what many thought was a quirky choice in actress Kirstin Dunst while rounding out the cast with the likes of Jason Schwartzman, Rip Torn, Judy Davis, Marianne Faithful and Asia Argento. As it turned out, the last role to be cast, that of Marie Antoinette's lover, Count Axel Fresen, was proving the most difficult.

Jamie speculated as to why in a *New York Times* interview. "I guess there had been pressure to have a certain ilk of actor, some big name actor from an up and coming list, but they hadn't been able to find someone."

On the surface, the character of Axel Fersen did not appear too taxing a transition from modeling to the silver screen. Essentially a glorified cameo, the character is only seen in a handful of scenes; riding in on horseback, attending a high society party, having some pretty randy sex with Marie Antoinette and then riding away. Jamie had to laugh at the fact that the first character he would be playing was little more than a male sex object. However, in taking time to research the real life character he would be portraying, he found much more in Axel Fersen to peek his interest.

"He was the richest man in Sweden at the time," Jamie enlightened *The Sunday Times*. "He was a soldier as well so it was nice to play somebody who's supposed to be really tough."

In any case, he was not in a position to be picky and so he flew to Paris and auditioned for Sofia. The consensus was that Jamie had done quite well but, this being the art house crowd, Jamie was not surprised that they would ask him back for a second audition. Jamie had those moments when the idea that he may well have botched yet another audition, ran rampant. The next afternoon he was told he had the part. And then it was time to celebrate.

"It was surreal," Jamie recalled in an *ASOS* interview. "I had drinks with Sofia and the producer at The Ritz in Paris. It was amazing. I thought every job would be like that."

Jamie was relaxed when he reported to the set of *Marie Antoinette*. He marveled at the logistics of a major motion picture, was prepared and managed to fuse his portrayal of the randy Count with nuances and moments that, to many observers, seemed lifted directly from his modeling experience, lingering looks and furtive glances. Having made his career primarily as a clothes horse, he found suddenly going from modern outfits to 18th century upper class costume an interesting change of pace. "I don't think I realized at the time how being in a costume helps with your performance," he told *What's On TV*.

In what was a lesser role, Jamie shined and, upon its release in 2006, critics, who were decidedly mixed on the finished product, seemed to be finding space to comment on Jamie's performance.

In typical Jamie fashion, he tossed off his *Marie Antoinette* experience with a heavy dose of nonchalance when he told *The Times*, "I thought it was all a bit of fun. I'd probably be better at it now."

For Jamie it was an important first step. Nobody could question that he seemed to have made a successful first step in a very limiting role. He was now confident that he had chosen the right profession and that there would most certainly be more to come.

Jamie would have a lot of time to contemplate his next acting move which, as he explained to *The Evening Herald* would be sometime in coming. "After Marie Antoinette there was a seven year gap without a lot of work. But I kept going because I truly wanted to be an actor."

Even though Keira and Jamie were now a thing of the past, there were those in the media who would look for even a fragment of speculation to rekindle the relationship in reader's minds. They found their angle early in 2006 when Sons of Jim unveiled some new songs at London's Teatro Club. Among the tunes was *Only On The Outside*, a tale of romance done in by outside forces that, to other than the casual listener, seemed a mournful blueprint as to how the pressures of celebrity had destroyed Jamie's relationship with Keira.

The tabloids ran with that story and, in what was becoming a more and more common occurrence, Jamie was once again faced with having to deny something. "Considering how David and I write together, I can't work out how it would be true," he told The Sunday Times.

But into 2006, one thing was becoming apparent. In the media's eyes he was now considered a star. Or, at the very least, somebody to keep an eye on.

CHAPTER EIGHT
OPEN SEASON

In the aftermath of his very public relationship and breakup with Keira, Jamie had become quite used to being tabloid and gossip friendly. And the way he dealt with it was to largely ignore it. When a prying reporter did corner him and ask for a comment on the latest sensationalist story surrounding him, he would categorically and often humorously deny it.

In Jamie's case going into a busy modeling season throughout most of 2006 and, consequently being surrounded by attractive models, made him a regular fixture in dating speculation circles. Shortly after a hectic early 2006, in which he jumped from ad campaigns for The Gap and Dior to magazine layouts for H&M and *L'Uomo Vogue*, Jamie reportedly had a brief fling with actress Sienna Miller. For Jamie it was a loose and non-pressure return to the dating world that only lasted a few dates, made some headlines and was quickly over.

Things became a little more dicey when the tabloids went wild with the fact that Jamie had a reportedly hot and heavy fling with that notorious train wreck Lindsay Lohan. This affair never really got beyond the ridiculous rumor stage as far as Jamie was concerned. But in the mind of Lindsay it was serious business, so much so that Jamie would be included some years later on a well - publicized list of that Lindsay created of all the Hollywood celebrities she had slept with.

March would see Jamie returning to the provocative world of Calvin Klein and going body to body with who many had long felt was his female equivalent on the modeling scene, Kate Moss. Their photo shoot for the latest campaign for Calvin Klein jeans would be every bit as daring if not more so. In it, a topless Kate would appear with her arms and other body parts wrapped around Jamie's equally visible torso and his Calvin's slung tight and low. It was a brazen attempt at sexuality to sell a clothing line and one, like Jamie's previous CK Jeans campaign, would have a long life on billboards, the sides of buses and an endless array of magazine spreads. Once again the division between art and exploitation was called into question in many critical corners. But to Jamie's way of thinking, it was a satisfying experience.

"There was a real buzz about the shoot," Jamie told Glamour. "To be part of it was amazing."

And the shoot also seemed to finally lay to rest the long simmering notion that Jamie was less than all man. Since he began modeling, Jamie had good naturedly endured an endless round of joking but biting comments from family and friends that being a model, despite the fame and the massive amounts of money, was less than a masculine occupation. But appearing topless with Kate seemed to silence the doubters as he offered in a *Glamour* piece.

"My mates mock me for doing this kind of work.

But once Kate came into the equation, they were suitably impressed."

Jamie's close proximity to Kate inevitably brought up the rumor that the two models were now romantically involved. Publications such as *Sex Degrees* breathlessly trumpeted the many Kate and Jamie sightings at various fashion functions and painted a picture of this latest item as the modeling super couple. At the silly end of the reportage, there was even speculation of what the offspring of a Jamie and Kate union might look like.

Jamie, in a humorous but candid comment, addressed the Kate dating rumors in a Just Jared report. "I'm not cool enough for her," he chuckled. "I've met her several times and she's really sweet. A lovely girl who is just so cool to be around. It's a nice thought of course. But somehow I don't think I'm cool enough or rock star enough. Given her taste in men, I'm really not her type."

With the conclusion of the Calvin Klein shoot, Jamie and David once again returned to the business of Sons of Jim. Jamie would be the first to admit that the group's early songs had been on the dark and dour side. And so in consort with songwriter Ali Thomson, they crafted a song entitled *My Burning Sun* which put forth a lighter and more positive message. The song was released on May 29, 2006, in conjunction with an EP of the same name, to positive response. As time permitted, Sons of Jim would continue to perform with much appreciated shows at The Islington Academy, a much anticipated and top flight show at Auntie Amme's in Belfast and support duty for New Zealand's favorite son Bic Runga at Dingwalls.

Late into 2006 and well into 2007, Jamie continued to be in demand and was constantly in front of a camera for some of the biggest brands in the fashion world. It had all become a blur and rather rote which continued to feed into his restlessness to give up modeling and devote himself fully to acting. However, with *Marie Antoinette* not hitting theaters until late in the year, very few people had seen Jamie on the big screen and could gauge his acting ability. With no new film opportunities in the offing Jamie, for better and for worse, was tied to his day job.

As one of the most famous models on the planet.

Through it all Jamie was continuing to keep it real. He would occasionally return to the rugby pitch for rough fun and games. He could be counted on to be at a club, lifting a pint with his close circle of friends, most of which still remembered him from back and the day and were quite capable of keeping their friend's head from getting too big with well-aimed barbs and drunken nights on the town.

Jamie's modeling assignments continued to make the world his playground and while in London on business, he made the acquaintance of yet another actress which would send the tabloid tongues a wagging.

Mischa Barton was in London, conducting business as the spokesperson for Keds Shoes, when she met Jamie. The particulars of how they met are almost non-existent. What little info there is on what must have been a particularly short-lived relationship was primarily photographic and consisted of a series of photos of the pair exiting an Arcade Fire concert. What is known, thanks to an item by *Sex Degrees* is that, when Jamie did not show up for a date, Mischa promptly ended the relationship. Jamie as a lout and a cad? It could be.

As 2007 neared its end, Sons of Jim was teetering on shaky ground. Universal Music Group had picked up the group's songs for distribution worldwide. Consequently David and Jamie were suddenly confronted with many aspects of the music business they were not prepared or inclined to deal with. There was also a matter of well- meaning producers and writers who, as Jamie would indirectly claim, were pulling them in a direction they did not necessarily want to go in.

In a bit of self-examination, Jamie confessed to *The Scotsman* that the band had finally run its course. "I didn't have a lot of belief in my personal capabilities," he said. "I eventually was not fulfilled by it. But we had a lot of good times."

Sons of Jim disbanded early in 2008.

CHAPTER NINE
AFTER A FEW DRINKS

Jamie knew a good idea when he heard one. Especially when the idea was presented after plenty of drinks at his sister's wedding party by a complete stranger who claimed to be a producer named Ben Grass. Once the party ended and Jamie had time to sober up, the idea still seemed pretty good.

Beyond The Rave proposed the story of a British soldier, about to ship out for Iraq, who spends his last night trying to track down his missing girlfriend who was last seen partying with a group of hardcore ravers. The ravers turn out to be vampires who are on a blood harvesting mission designed to sustain them during an upcoming sea voyage. The soldier tracks the vampire clan down and, with the aid of several non - bloodsucking ravers, deals out lethal and bloody revenge on the undead. Yes it was B movie all the way but *Beyond The Rave* had two things going for it. It was planned as a 20-part horror serial that would be released first as a digital download and, shortly thereafter, as the first official release of the recently relaunched Hammer Films, the legendary horror house that Christopher Lee and Peter Cushing built.

Jamie acknowledged that initial meeting in a conversation with Interview. "I met the producer at my sister's wedding party and was very fond of him. I liked what he was trying to do with the project and, after plenty of drinks, I said I'd like to be involved."

For his part, producer Grass, was equally impressed with Jamie as he explained in a *Fangoria* interview. "I enjoyed him in *Marie Antoinette* and was aware that he wanted to do more acting. Jamie has a wonderful way of connecting with young audiences and he blew us away at the audition."

Jamie was hired to play Ed, the soldier turned vampire fighter, and immediately found himself in a different kind of working environment. *Marie Antoinette* had been a moderately budgeted studio picture complete with a leisurely shoot. *Beyond The Rave* was extremely low budget with a tight number of shooting days. And although his work in the aforementioned period film was diverse enough to show his talents, *Beyond The Rave* was largely action and physical conflict, something Jamie, as sedate model, was not used to.

"It was a mad shoot," he recalled in Interview. "The whole shoot was a night shoot. I was sleeping all day, having no life, then getting up, going to work at six in the evening and coming home at six in the morning. I don't remember a great deal about that time through a lack of sleep."

But what he did recall in an interview with Scene Junkie was the surreal nature of it all. "We were in a rave sequence that was cool and all of a sudden there's vampires and a lot of running around and I've got lines to say. After a while you sort of forgot that you were in a movie."

Jamie's acting ambitions were now in high gear with the completion of *Beyond The Rave*. would continue throughout 2008, occasionally interrupted by modeling assignments. In a sense the modeling had become a highly lucrative blur of cameras and positions. He was quite capable at this point of striking the required pose without being asked. And truth be known, for Jamie it was getting boring, and yes, too much like work, established and content on the surface while his ego continued to take a beating with the job title of Male Model.

"I definitely don't love modeling," he said in an interview that appeared in Boston.com and other outlets. "I never did. I mean I have respect for it, that's fine. But I've never gone 'oh yes I'm a model'. I think it sounds ridiculous for a man to say that."

Consequently, when his drive to develop acting attention was not forthcoming from the big boys, he turned his attention to the short film where there were opportunities available if he was willing to work for nothing or next to nothing.

Not long after *Beyond The Rave*, Jamie found himself co- starring in a psychologically demanding little film called *Nice To Meet You*. The intimate drama, which co-starred Trudie Styler (wife of rocker Sting) and Mickey Sumner (daughter of Sting) in a 20-minute odyssey of emotional twists and turns in which a woman is suddenly startled by a young man jumping over her fence into her backyard. He claims he is being chased by the police and begs the woman to hide him. Sexual tension immediately develops only to be interrupted by the arrival of the woman's daughter. A few days later the daughter returns with her boyfriend, the man the woman had hidden. As the unsuspecting daughter and the young man prepare to leave, the young man slips the mother a note indicating that, all his flaws aside, they will meet again.

For anyone who has seen *Nice To Meet You*, it is evident that Jamie is playing very much to both his own personality as well as the image he has projected in his modeling; alternately brooding, youthful and sexually tense. Less a stereotype and caricature than a flesh and blood character, Jamie's portrayal in this very small film was easily his best acting work to date.

Jamie was keen to showcase his versatility as an actor and the opportunity to do something light years removed from *Nice To Meet You* came with the lead role in an action packed action/adventure spectacular, clocking in at 11 minutes, entitled *X Returns*.

The plot, big on science fiction and even bigger on running, jumping and the spectacle of Jamie, as the mysteriously titled Agent X, snarling with a gun in his hand, backstories Jamie's character as an Apollo astronaut on a super- secret mission who returns to earth infected with an alien virus. He is immediately whisked away to what turns out to be a forty year prison sentence in which he is subjected to cruel scientific testing. Finally after forty years of this, Agent X escapes his confinement and is soon racing through Los Angeles, pursued by his captors, as he attempts to discover what happened to his family and his past life while learning the real secrets of his imprisonment.

As silly, and as predictable as this all sounds, the movie is a kinetic, action-packed thrill ride that showcases Jamie's abilities as an everyman action star, fully capable of the handful of human moments as well as the manly action. *X Returns* would go on to win a handful of film festival awards while satisfactorily expanding Jamie's acting resume to include action hero.

In 2009 Jamie would finally break through to his second full length feature and his first sustained co-starring role in the low budget, character driven *Shadows In the Sun* in which he plays a mysterious younger man and helpmate to an elderly woman who helps bring her together with her estranged son and his children. *Shadows In the Sun* was attractive to Jamie for a number of reasons. The role was a full bodied flesh and blood character rather than a caricature. But of equal importance was the opportunity to work opposite legendary actress Jean Simmons who had not worked in more than ten years and, as fate would have it, *Shadows In the Sun* would be her last work before her passing.

Those who observed the shoot were instantly drawn to the warm and believable relationship Jamie projected in his scenes with Simmons. It would be a working and personal relationship that Jamie would remember fondly years later in a conversation with Interview that, reportedly, brought tears to his eyes.

"She was one of my favorite people in the world. *Shadows In the Sun* was her last film. She was the most incredible person. She had amazing stories and was a joy to be around."

Jamie's on the job training continued on *Shadows In the Sun*. His part offered much more depth and it resulted in a full-bodied performance that, in all honesty, most critics doubted a model turned actor was capable of. When not in front of the camera, Jamie was open and friendly with cast and crew alike and learning the importance of being a part of a creative team rather than a diva.

Encouraged by his earliest film roles, Jamie was fantasizing about giving up modeling for good and plunging full bore into acting. But ever the pragmatist, he knew that he was still the most popular male model on the planet and, yes, what he had made thus far as an actor would barely pay his rent. And so, while he anticipated the next acting role that might well make his career, he knew that the next phone call would most likely be to strip down to his skivvies once again for massive amounts of cash.

One of the more memorable modeling excursions in 2009 would turn out to be the highly oiled up and erotic Calvin Klein underwear and jeans campaign with actress/model Eva Mendes. Following on the heels of the Kate Moss campaign, the Mendes shoot was ultra- sexualized and typically controversial. Even the most positive reviews of the campaign had to admit that the images of Eva and Jamie scantily clad and draped all over each other were, in the best possible way were sexy and dirty.

But the comments the two models made that appeared in the *Stupid Celebrities* website made it clear that they were thrilled to have done it. "Calvin Klein jeans and underwear are both such iconic American brands that to play a part in this campaign was a true honor," said Jamie. His partner in modeling crime, Mendes, cut to the chase. "I had a great time on set with Jamie."

Not unexpectedly the marketing campaign, in

keeping with Calvin Klein's track record, was a massive success and Jamie was even further entrenched as a major model with a few minor acting credits. It was an image that Jamie would continue to fight as he offered in *British Vogue*.

"I will always think of myself during that time as being a relatively successful model and more of a failed actor.

And like it or not, going into 2010, this was Jamie's life.

CHAPTER TEN
HOT AND HUMILIATING

The modeling world was not making it easy for Jamie to say no. While the acting opportunities post *Shadows In the Sun* had dwindled to less than zero, modeling brands were continuing to beat down his door.

Calvin Klein loved Jamie. So much so that they gave Jamie a three year contract, a rarely offered deal usually reserved for only the top models that would keep him busy and, needless to say, well off for the immediate future.

But the terms of the deal also allowed Jamie to work elsewhere when not employed by Calvin Klein and his modeling agency was quick to line up outside work. One was a typically daring and somewhat provocative layout with French Vogue that had him romping for the camera with model Natasha Poly. An unusual break from the erotically charged campaigns that had become Jamie's bread and butter was the *Vogue Hommes Magazine* layout in which Jamie, with the exception of one scene in which he is looking lovingly at a small child, had the model in solitary repose in indoor and outdoor locations looking alone and disconsolate in ruggedly, classically, he man outfits.

Jamie's interest was considerably peaked when Calvin Klein announced that they were reuniting Eva and he for another photo shoot destined to highlight the 2010 jeans line. Jamie, in his patented laidback way, made no bones about the fact that he had a bit of a mad crush on Mendes in an interview with *Bang Showbiz*.

"She's great fun to be around. She's very sexy. I'd say she's the perfect template of how every woman should look."

The latest ad campaign was as equally hot, sexy and greased down as the previous year's had been and, not surprisingly, gave rise to the rumor that Jamie and Eva were secretly an item. It was a rumor they chose to ignore although Jamie did acknowledge at one point that being romantically linked to the model's he's worked with has become an annual rite of not true.

Jamie's UK based talent agency, United Talent Agency, had been doing their best to find acting jobs for their client with only marginal results. In 2010 they decided that expanding Jamie's profile by sending him to Los Angeles to audition for Pilot Season might be a good way to go. Pilot Season is the annual meat and meet market fest in which actors come to audition for television pilots that have been green lighted for production. The hope among actors is, ideally, to land a part in a pilot that ultimately gets picked up for the fall television season and, even better, is a ratings success that would ultimately ensure the actor of a long and lucrative run on television that, in many cases, could be a career maker.

Jamie agreed to go but not without the usual plea that he had never been very good at auditioning and selling himself. "I failed a fucking hundred of them," he told the London Evening Standard. "Some of them were totally humiliating experiences."

But it was an opportunity to see Hollywood in action and, he felt, maybe he would get lucky. Unfortunately, by the time he landed in Los Angeles, his reputation, both good and bad, had preceded him.

Word quickly spread that the model who had done those legendary Calvin Klein underwear ads was in town, trying to become an actor. That he also had a handful of film credits did not seem to factor into the equation. Jamie was about to run head first into casting bias.

"People attach too much to the idea of being a model," he explained to *The London Evening Standard* in referencing his audition days in Los Angeles. "In their eyes you're an actor who used to be a model never trained to be an actor. There were not many directors lining up."

Consequently Pilot Season for Jamie, according to comments in *The Telegraph*, "was one of the most dehumanizing things anyone could ever go through." It was an ordeal made all the more painful for the actor by what he claimed was the amount of bad scripts and story ideas he had to wade through on the road to often abrupt dismissals.

"I read some really awful stuff," he recalled to *This Is London*. "I could have very easily ended up in something rubbish. You just get lucky if you get something good."

Jamie was always a quick study and, in the case of

Pilot Season, he was quick to pick up on how the Los Angeles casting process soothed actor's egos. "In Los Angeles I've only had what they call 'the silent no's'," he chuckled in a *Sunday Times* interview. "There's no such thing as a bad meeting in Los Angeles. You always walk out thinking that you have the job."

When not auditioning, Jamie attempted some limited sightseeing and, along the way, fell in with a couple of other hopeful actors, Andrew Garfield and Eddie Redmayne. Nobody had much money so the high life was out of the question. But as Redmayne would recall years later in a conversation with Variety, they did quite well by using their wits.

"We used to go to The Standard Hotel in West Hollywood and split a sandwich because that meant we could get cheaper parking. We would swim and play table tennis for hours."

Jamie was thoroughly enjoying the idea of being free and easy and living on the edge and jokingly relished the experience in an article that appeared in the website *Jamie Dornan Life*. "Six years ago we were whoring around Los Angeles. We had no scripts, no women in our lives and very little dignity."

Jamie put the best possible face on Pilot Season, dutifully wandering in and out of rooms where often impromptu auditions with little or no warning would typically take place. As his time in Los Angeles was winding down, Jamie was resigned to return to London without an acting job but confident that his modeling career would always be there. In his darkest moments, once he was finished, dissected what he considered the inanity of Pilot Season, he realized that he was just part of a very big pack trying to stand out.

It was at that moment he was handed a script for something called *Once Upon A Time*. He read the pages with interest, especially the ones marked for a particular character that the producers were dangling in front of him.

He liked what he saw.

CHAPTER ELEVEN
AND THEN YOU DIE

At first blush *Once Upon A Time* was nothing to sneeze at. The two executive producers and creators, Adam Horowitz and Edward Kitsis, had cut their teeth as writers on the television series *Lost* and the movie *Tron: Legacy* so it was a safe bet that *Once Upon A Time* would not be the latest bit of predictable television fare.

The premise of *Once Upon A Time* sets up in a fictional seaside town called Storybrooke, a mysterious place where the residents are actually characters from fairytales who have been transported to the town and robbed of their real memories by a powerful curse. The structure of each one hour episode was equally quirky in that a main storyline is set in the town while a secondary backstory focuses on a character's life before the curse was enacted.

Among the huge, ala *Lost*, ensemble cast, Jamie was handed the role of Sheriff Graham Humbert whose fairytale alter ego is The Huntsman.

Jamie readily accepted the opportunity, all the while his shyness and basic insecurities were racing through his mind. He had never done series television before and was not sure how he would adjust to the daily and weekly grind of it all. But Jamie need have only thought of the alternative being his current day job to mentally put any doubts aside.

Jamie reported to Vancouver, Canada for the shooting of the pilot. Jamie made fast friends with the cast and crew and was excited to be part of something that, if it went to series, would be seen by millions. But he knew that only a small percentage of pilots make it to series and that the only people who might see his performance might well be the ones who turned thumbs down on the show. However the vibe on the set was positive and it would become even more so not long after when *Once Upon A Time* was announced as part of the 2011 fall television schedule.

It was then that the producers dropped the bombshell.

"When we finally started shooting the series, I was told that my character was going to die before the end of the first season," he told *E*. "It was a bit of a shock but there I was and we still had so many episodes to film."

For the next four months, Jamie and the cast of *Once Upon A Time* went about the business of churning out first season episodes. It was not long before the rest of the cast and crew were told that Jamie's character was literally dead man walking. Jamie, in hindsight with E, acknowledged that the situation was odd, going to work each day with the knowledge that his days were numbered.

"It was strange getting to bond with everyone while knowing this (the death) was coming," he said. "We were all together for four months and building great friendships while knowing all the while that the end for me was coming."

But that did not prevent Jamie from doing solid work in what would be a total of eight episodes. Beginning with the Pilot episode, Sheriff Graham proves an alternately by the book and insightful character who is at the center of setting the stories and conflicts into motion, especially as it pertains to the character of Emma who is an unwilling visitor to Storybrooke. In the episode entitled *Snow Falls*, Jamie's Sheriff Graham joins Emma and Mary Margaret as they search the woods for the mysterious, injured John Doe whose alter ego is Prince Charming.

Once Upon A Time premiered in October 2011. From the outset, the show was pulling good ratings and a rapidly expanding fandom made up of people who live and die by fantasy worlds and, by association, veteran television junkies who saw marked similarities between *Once Upon A Time* and *Lost*.

During those early episodes the producers saw Jamie's Sheriff Graham as a potential breakout character despite his impending demise and were quick to work in a subtle power struggle between Sheriff Graham and Regina whose fairytale identity will turn out to be The Evil Queen. Jamie looked back on that conflict in a conversation with *The Hollywood Reporter*.

"In Season One, we see the fact that Regina is in control of him [Graham] and getting what she wants from him. Poor Graham, he's just doing what he's told. He doesn't have the conscience to fight against it."

Inside Grey's Anatomy: The Unauthorized Biography of Jamie Dornan

As the episodes of Once Upon A Time played out, Jamie would admit that the knowledge that his character's days were numbered was beginning to do a number on his head, despite the fact that he was showcasing diverse acting chops and showing potential employers that, yes, he could indeed act. There were the inevitable on set rumors and speculation that the producers were having a change of heart and were trying frantically to figure out a way to keep Jamie's character. Sadly for Jamie, the talk would be just that.

"The weird thing always weighing in the back of my mind was that 'the episode was getting closer and closer," he explained to *Digital Spy*. "You basically start trying to adjust to that fact."

The storyline that would inevitably lead to Graham's death began to develop and, by episode seven, *The Heart Is a Lonely Hunter*, the time had come.

"When we filmed Season One, Graham was almost settled into his role as Regina's puppet," he recalled to *The Hollywood Reporter*. "He's been doing what she says for so long that, by episode seven, he starts to realize some things. He questions it, talks back to her, confronts her and goes against her. It ends up backfiring because she kills him."

And Graham's death was nothing if not unexpected, gruesome and, in a way, in keeping with the *Once Upon A Time* vibe. Graham finally expresses his feelings for Emma. As they kiss, Regina appears, reaches into a mystic box, pulls out Graham's heart and crushes it. Graham collapses and dies at her feet. Jamie would look back on the death of Sheriff Graham with a mixture of sadness and gallows humor when speaking to *Digital Spy*.

"The death was pretty gruesome but it was also a little bit cool. Not many people get to die like that. As television deaths go, I was pretty happy."

Not so happy were the legions of *Once Upon A Time* fans who had quickly taken the character of Sheriff Graham to their collective bosoms. Jamie took the mini-backlash as a compliment or sorts and was quick to point out to *Digital Spy* that the very makeup of *Once Upon A Time*, in which each character has a real world and fairytale character, meant that Jamie might be gone but not necessarily forever.

"This is the last you'll see of Sheriff Graham but I'm not sure this is the last you'll see of my face on the show," he teased. "My fairytale character [The Huntsman] does not die and so there will always be that option."

As it turned out that option was very much on the minds of the show's creators as *Once Upon A Time* chugged along to good ratings and betting odds favoring the show's renewal for a second season. Even though Sheriff Graham's demise had been a foregone conclusion since the show began, they were not blind to the backlash and support for Jamie's Graham and/or The Huntsman to somehow make an appearance. Horowitz and Kitsis mulled over the possibilities and finally at a San Diego Comic Con interview, the producers announced that they had found a way to bring Jamie back as The Huntsman for the Season One finale entitled *A Land without Magic*.

In the storyline, Prince Charming is searching for Snow White when he is suddenly surrounded by the masked guards of The Evil Queen. Things don't look good for the Prince. When suddenly one of the masked guards begins shooting his arrows into his own men. In dramatic fashion, the guard whips off his mask to reveal The Huntsman. It was a brief but dramatic return but it gave hope to the show's fans that, in the world of *Once Upon A Time*, anything was truly possible.

For his part, Jamie was quick with the platitudes when he told reporters it was good to be back, albeit briefly, with his old friends and how Vancouver was still Vancouver and the sets were pretty much as he had left them. Jamie pointed out that not much had changed since the moment when The Evil Queen had quite literally broken his heart.

But the reality was that, for Jamie, quite a bit had.

Post his character's demise, Jamie was once again cast adrift as an unemployed actor in search of a job. And it gave him the opportunity to assess his life and career to that point. While modeling had turned him into a celebrity and made him quite well off financially, all the Calvin Klein and associated modeling jobs on his resume could not distract from the reality that his modeling career had been nothing more than luck.

"It was all a fluke," he candidly told *The Sun*. "I was not the best looking guy who was doing that job. I just got lucky. I knew I wanted to act and was always trying to find my way into it while modeling. But there were always other distractions. I was still involved in modeling and was still mucking around trying to be in a band. But I always knew that I wanted to be an actor."

And so Jamie decided early in 2012 to devote all his efforts into acting. Not that he was suddenly thrust into the unemployment weeds without a compass. Jamie still had the luxury of some high end modeling contracts that would keep him afloat and he was not above taking the odd one off job if it interested him in some way.

But from now on Jamie's job description would read Jamie Dornan: Actor.

CHAPTER TWELVE
ALL FALL

If Jamie had a preference, it would have been to jump immediately in a solid motion picture role, something with depth and character, something that would get him noticed. The last thing he wanted was a second go round at Hollywood Pilot Season. When it was suggested, on the heels of his positive response in *Once Upon A Time*, that trying his luck once again with television might be the way to go, mentally kicking and screaming all the way across the Atlantic, he nevertheless gave it another shot.

And immediately found himself knee deep in stereotypes.

Jamie's profile, thanks to *Once Upon A Time*, had put him higher up the Hollywood pecking order but the result, as the actor once again wandered in and out of casting sessions, admittedly giving less than stellar auditions, was pretty much more of the same. He was dealing with highly derivative takes on his *Once Upon A Time* character without the passion and substance. And being on a hit television series, even for his short period, had not erased the notion of Jamie as model turned actor which brought with it laughable, to his way of thinking, offers.

"You do read so much shit," he offered in a *Red* interview, "and a lot of that might have had a lot to do with the fact that I modeled. Usually (what I was being offered) is the character that, two pages before the end, kisses the girl and that's it."

Jamie was utterly fatigued, deflated and unemployed as he hopped a plane back to London at the end of Pilot Season. His plane had barely touched down in the UK when an offer to audition for something very British and very different came his way. A BBC 2 thriller called *The Fall*.

The Fall, which toplines Gillian (*The X Files*) Anderson as veteran officer Stella Gibson, is a filmed in Belfast crime thriller about a London police investigator who is brought to Belfast to investigate a growing series of murders of young professional women. We discover early on that the killer is Paul Spector, a happily-married husband and father who, by day, works as a Bereavement Counselor and, by night, becomes the worst sort of killer. Far from a straight ahead whodunit, The Fall focuses on all facets of the investigator and killer's lives that is just as much character driven as tension packed and horrific.

The Fall, created and written by Allan Cubitt, had been in various degrees of development since 2010 and Anderson had been officially on board since the beginning of 2012. Originally Jamie would be auditioning for the secondary role of a police officer, a role her perceived as an interesting turn that would provide him with different opportunities to test his acting skills.

Perhaps fatigued from his second grind in

Hollywood and fearing he would not get far with a standard audition tape, Jamie, with tongue planted firmly in cheek, chose a rather unorthodox approach

"I saw Jamie's audition tape," *Fall* creator Cubitt told Stylist. "It was just Jamie peeling an orange. It was very clear from that tape that Jamie was the guy."

But not necessarily that guy. Cubitt was known for thinking outside the box when it came to casting and the minute he saw Jamie's audition tape, his contrary antenna went up. Suddenly he saw Jamie as the killer. Cubitt's thinking did not stop there. For the first time in Jamie's career, it had not even dawned on Cubitt that Jamie was good-looking.

During his initial audition for the police officer, something in his quiet nature and upfront physicality jumped out at Cubitt and Jamie was asked to audition again, this time for the serial killer Spector. As Jamie quickly perused the script pages for his second audition, he knew going in that the role was far from cliché. He would be required to alternately be the domestic loving family man and the diabolical killer. And while he had never done a British-based series before, he had watched enough to know that they were atypical and often darkly progressive in their approach to long traditional genre tropes.

Jamie felt he was ready to tackle *The Fall* on the day he showed up for his audition. But at the end of the day, Jamie felt he had, once again, not done real well and was ready to chalk up another loss as he walked out the door. His chances were also hurt by the fact that, even as he was auditioning to play the worst kind of psychological monster, all people seemed to notice was how attractive he was. But luckily, *Fall* creator Allan Cubitt was notorious for thinking differently.

"I guess I saw his potential and didn't let anything stand in my way," Cubitt said in remarks that appeared in *British Vogue* and *Ten News*. "You only need to meet Jamie once to realize he has a huge amount going for him beyond being physically attractive."

To Cubitt's way of thinking, Jamie was ideal for the role of Spector. Now all he had to do was convince everybody else, a primarily the executives at BBC 2 that Jamie being amazingly attractive and a former model did not mean that he did not have talent.

For his part, the ever cautious Jamie was somewhat bemused at the idea that he had even made it this far in the casting process. "I was a risk and I was totally aware of it," he told *The Times*. "I had never been a lead in anything. I'm sure I wasn't on anyone's short list when they started thinking about casting. I would doubt that I was even on a long list."

Anderson ironically recalled in *Red* that they "made Jamie jump through hoops" during an extended and arduous casting process. "The initial intention was not to hire somebody who was that attractive," the actress related to *In Style*. "However it was clear from the beginning that he was the man for the job. It didn't have anything to do with his good looks although, in the process, we realized what that would do psychologically to the viewer and there was something intriguing about that."

Anderson's notion became reality during one pivotal audition sequence in which Jamie who, as Spector, had just returned from a voyeuristic/fetish kind of burglary that would set up his next victim, returns home in time for a tender moment with his children. Show creator Allan Cubitt acknowledged in The Telegraph what made Jamie stand out from the pack in this particularly complex scene.

"Some people were playing it (the scene) as if he wanted to murder a child. But Jamie came in and spoke kindly to the boy and kissed his daughter goodnight. That was much more disconcerting to the audience."

And it also turned out to be the source of disagreement between Jamie and the show's creator Allan Cubitt, as related by Jamie in *Grazia Italy*. "Allan argued that a serial killer could not love his own children. But I think it's important to tell that side of the story." Jamie would win that battle and ultimately the war.

The final look at Jamie would entail a marathon six hour audition in which Jamie would perform various aspects of the Paul Spector character for Cubitt and others who ultimately held a big career step in their hands. By the time it was over, Jamie, not surprisingly, was showing all the signs of cabin fever.

"I felt like I had fucking earned it (the role)," he told *The London Evening Standard*. "I worked my dick off for that role."

Jamie was officially announced as the killer in *The Fall* in February 2012. By March he had literally gone home again when *The Fall* began four months of shooting in Belfast. But Jamie's sense of coming full circle was colored by his taking on his most challenging role to date, a man of two characters whose true evil is balanced by moments of real tenderness.

That the series would be shot in Belfast also gave the actor an opportunity to return to his roots. He took an apartment in the center of town, in close proximity to family and friends. But when not on the set, Jamie would find often revert to being alone. A non-working day would usually find Jamie getting up at a reasonable hour, picking up newspapers and repairing to a local café where he would spend the day reading. And, among his thoughts, was the amazement that he had gotten the part. Point of fact, Jamie was so insecure during those early days of filming that he acknowledged several times that he felt he would be fired at any moment.

"I thought I was in over my head when they cast me," he confessed to *Radio Times*. "It was tough and not an easy place to have your head in."

However Jamie was nothing if not diligent in wanting to get Paul Spector right. He would pour over countless books and videos chronicling the exploits of serial killers. And he was quick to understand what made The Fall something truly out of the ordinary.

"Within the first five minutes of the opening episode you know it's Paul Spector," he revealed to *Radio Times*. "You get to live with him and follow him and get to see the why rather than the who."

Jamie had never pretended to be anything approaching a method actor, preferring a much more natural approach to acting that allow him to do his acting chore and then, just as quickly, slip back into being just Jamie.

As the first days on the set passed, Jamie, when not in character, was an easy mix with the rest of the cast and crew who, to a person, saw him as a calm, level head and down to earth person.

"Jamie is one of the most grounded people I know," his co-star Andersen told *Red*. "He's got it all in perspective and has a very appropriate and right sized take on all of this."

Actress Bronagh Waugh, who plays Spector's unsuspecting wife in *The Fall* recalled in a *Heat* conversation that while Jamie and she got on well "No one really knew who Jamie was at that point." Jamie's anonymity in the outside world, despite his extensive modeling experience and his short lived popularity on *Once Upon A Time*, was palpable and it went hand in hand with his lingering discomfort with celebrity and being in the public eye. It was a point driven home shortly after filming began when Bronagh and Jamie, in an attempt to bond with the actors playing their children, had an outing at the zoo. Bronagh, by this time a veteran actress with the television series *Hollyoaks* under her belt was immediately recognized by zoo patrons and hounded for pictures and autographs while Jamie went totally unrecognized.

"At one point Jamie turned to me and said 'this is so weird.'" Related Bronagh to *Heat*. "He was so shy and self-deprecating about it. I turned to him and said 'Yeah if the show is a success you're going to have to get used to it.'"

Although Jamie and Anderson would appear in very few scenes together during that first season, it was a given that Anderson, who had seen it all and had a reputation for not suffering fools or prima donnas lightly, would be the person Jamie would have to look and act his best in front of. She acknowledged as much in *British Vogue*. "He's very funny and he has a good singing voice. I mean I tried really hard to find something wrong with him."

Another cast member, Karen Hassan, was succinct in her impressions of Jamie in a *Belfast Telegraph* conversation. "He's lovely, a real gentleman."

Jamie would downplay the notion of his turning into the class clown in *The Fall* when he explained to a BBC interviewer "I'd love to become a prankster. But no I'm not hiding things in Gillian's trailer or anything like that. I like to have a laugh and I can get very silly and can make jokes that will not be funny to anyone but me."

And because of that, when it was time to slip into his role of killer, he would suffer guilt pangs when committing his vile acts against people he had, only moments earlier, presented himself as easy going Jamie. And as he explained on *The Graham Norton Show*, albeit in a humorous manner, it made for some legitimate turmoil.

"I was doing the creepiest things imaginable to my co-stars and making them very uncomfortable," he said "and so I kept apologizing to them. It wasn't easy for them and I was very aware of how horrible it was and so I kept saying 'I'm sorry' during horrible scenes."

Equally challenging and somewhat draining during the making of *The Fall* was the fact that Jamie was often put in the position of filming a warm family moment right before he turned diabolical as he staked out his next victim. Jamie would admit on *The Graham Norton Show* and *Radio Times* that his normally laidback, far from violent nature, often took a beating as the scenes unfolded.

"This doesn't come easy to me," he offered. "It's

a brutal head space to maintain and so I made a point of getting out of character. I didn't want to be taking Spector home."

He would also have those days when he would read the script pages for the day and wish he could call in sick. "Any scene where you're straddling an actress with tights around her neck and me with a very mean looking face doesn't make for an easy day at the office," he told *Heat*. "There were plenty of those scenes."

Mental issues were not the only ones challenging Jamie during *The Fall*. The very nature of Paul Spector, as envisioned by Cubitt, was very introverted and wound up tight. There was no room for anything in his makeup that rang of adrenaline fused, which ran contrary to Jamie's always moving, always doing something attitude. It immediately became apparent that Jamie would need an outlet and so, in between scenes, he could often be found walking in endless circles, walking up and down studio corridors and, on occasion, screaming at the top of his lungs. It must have been a shock to see Jamie thrashing around physically. But, after a time, the show's cast and crew most certainly chalked it up to 'oh that's just Jamie' and went about their business.

As Jamie got deeper and deeper into the production he discovered that, in fact, despite its brooding and dark nature, the role of Spector had turned out to be quite the physical workout as well. The way his killer methodically stalked and then killed his victims required constant, subtle body movements and it was no small secret that Jamie was managing to stay in good physical shape.

Jamie was willing to do anything that the scripts had declared for optimum dramatic effect. And that attitude included doing what many on *The Fall* creative team considered the most disturbing and boundary pushing sequence of the entire first season. Jamie matter of factly tossed off the grotesque particulars in a conversation with *Digital Spy*.

"I spent a day strangling myself on the back of a door while I masturbated to a driver's license of one of my victims. That's not an easy day at the office. And then they cut it [the scene] out and didn't even tell me."

The Fall completed filming for its full season in June 2012 with a compelling cliffhanger that would, hopefully, prime the pump for a second season. Although it would ultimately be almost a year before the first season would make its May 2013 debut, the production company was ecstatic with what they had shot and, in particular, the cool and enticing chemistry that had developed between Jamie and Andersen. Jamie was particularly anxious for *The Fall* to debut as he acknowledged in conversation with *The Belfast Telegraph*.

"Very few people who watch BBC dramas would know I was a model. I'm keen for this to come out because I think it might change things a little bit."

CHAPTER THIRTEEN
JAMIE'S IN LOVE

Jamie and Amelia sat down in a comfortable couch. He put a tape in the television. As the television flickered on, they sat close. Jamie was tense. This would be the first time Amelia had seen her fiancé in his role of serial killer Paul Spector. It would be a test of his acting ability. But, more importantly, it would be a test of their trust and their relationship.

Amelia was about to see the man she loved as a monster.

It was not like they had not known this moment was coming. Amelia sensed that *The Fall* was important to him and that it could prove a turning point in his career. And so she had been more than willing to help. Dornan reported in a *Daily Star* piece that Amelia was instrumental in helping Jamie research the role, literally staying up all night in bed with her lover as he studiously studied the myriad of books of the morbid subject matter of serial killers.

But this night things were different. They sat silent as Paul Spector went about his violent business as a serial killer and his domestic moments as a family man. They both sat transfixed as the drama and the horror played out, Jamie most likely casting furtive glances at Amelia, looking for something to gauge her reaction.

After the television went to black Jamie would recall that there was silence and some tense moments as Amelia wrapped her thoughts around what she had just seen. Jamie was quite good as an actor which made her feelings at the moment all the more difficult. For a short period of time there would be some shakiness and a hint of some trust issues. But ultimately Amelia was alright with it.

Amelia had been an actress for the better part of ten years. She knew the business and had a firm grip on the difference between fiction and fact…

And the fact was that she knew the man she loved.

By the time Jamie had gotten over the hard knocks of his very public relationship with Keira and the endless rumors and innuendo surrounding Sienna Miller, Kate Moss and just about every woman he had personal or professional contact with, Jamie had gone completely underground when it came to women. It's a safe bet that Jamie had not been a monk going into 2009. But it was a safe bet that if anything of a romantic or even lustful nature was going on, Jamie was taking great pains to keep it private.

In 2009, Jamie was at a Hollywood party when he was introduced by friends to Amelia Warner. Amelia had grown up in a show business family and, not surprisingly, had gravitated toward acting and music at a fairly young age. Amelia moved up the acting ladder from the Royal Court Theater Group to several BBC productions, including an adaptation of Lorna Doone and a wide variety of studio and independent films that included *Quills, Mansfield Park, Aeon Flux* and *What a Girl Wants*.

Amelia was also capable of a spontaneous and wild side. During a previous relationship with actor Colin Farrell, the couple reportedly decided to get married during a holiday in Tahiti. She was quick to clarify the story in a conversation with *The Sun*. "We had a ceremony on a beach in Tahiti that was by no means legal and knew it wasn't. It was just a thing we did on holiday."

Like Jamie, Amelia was quietly and intellectually inclined. She was not afraid to speak her mind She was somebody with a sense of humor. And to Jamie's way of thinking she was very feminine. The pair hit it off almost immediately and, into 2010, were seeing each other exclusively.

Why the relationship would remain under the radar was open to conjecture. One reason was that both were quite busy in their own careers; in the case of Amelia she was busy establishing a minor music career, under the name Slow Moving Millie, that produced two minor hits, *Beasts* and a clever Smiths cover *Please, Please Me Let Me Get What I Want*. And speculation was that when they were together, it was often in either out of the way locations or together in a quiet setting.

And while dual careers and long periods apart had been the death knell for uncounted relationships, Jamie was effusive some years later in an *Entertainmentwise* article in giving his, by this time, wife Amelia the lion's share of the credit for avoiding that pitfall. "Well my wife is a brilliant understanding person. Plus she was an actress for ten years so she knows what it [the business] is like."

They were both avid readers, as witness the fact that the computer generated version of *The Guardian* was marked as a favorite app and one they reportedly looked at first thing after getting up. No matter the reason, Jamie and Amelia were rarely in the paparazzi's lens and then little was made of it. Because when they were out and about, it barely seemed to register beyond the fact that here was a typical young couple out on the streets or running errands.

And when they were spotted it was often in a hand holding, lingering looks mode. It was clear to even the casual observer that Jamie and Amelia were very much in love. In 2011, Jamie and Amelia made the tabloid press in the best possible way…

…When they announced that they were engaged to be married.

CHAPTER FOURTEEN
TWO FOR THE SHOW

Barely into 2013 and a good five months before it was set to make its television debut, the buzz behind *The Fall* was cooking on an extremely high heat. And in particular, special notice was being taken of Jamie's steely performance as the serial killer and devoted family man.

Predictably, scenes and/or episodes of *The Fall* were being 'leaked' to press to prime the pump for the release. But in an even more stealth manner, people of note who had worked on *The Fall* were also getting the word out in informal conversation and, in the case of the first season director Jakob Verbruggen, it meant getting some footage to his good friend, fellow director Dominique Deruddere.

Deruddere was a well-known European/art house director who was about to try his hand at a more traditional romantic comedy entitled *Flying Home* (whose title would be changed to *Racing Hearts* upon release). The story focuses on a young and quite mercenary New York financial executive who, in order to close an important deal with bird racing obsessed Dubai Sheik, must secure a particular racing pigeon whose owner lives in a remote Flemish village. The executive concocts a plan to go to the village and, under the guise of a school teacher searching for records of a long lost relative, and convince the owner to sell him the pigeon. As the story plays out, the executive has an emotional and personal change of heart as he falls under the spell of the village and the owner's granddaughter. On the surface, *Flying Home* appeared to be a cookie cutter romantic dramedy, seemingly safe considering the director's body of work, but as Deruddere would explain, it was a deeper story that ultimately focused on love, loss and the human price that people often pay for freedoms and liberties.

For the pivotal role of Colin, the financial executive, the director had been looking for a specific kind of actor and, as he explained in the film's press notes, he was having a hard time finding that actor. "The actor we wanted for the role of Colin had to be someone who would have to portray the reversal of a ruthless businessman," said Deruddere. "I received a lot of resumes and tapes but no one appeared to have that second layer. That's when my friend Jakob Verbruggen sent me some scenes of Jamie in *The Fall*. Jamie had more than his pretty boy look first revealed. Seeing those scenes from *The Fall* were decisive to me in my decision. The young fashion model turned out to be a solid actor."

Jamie had reached a point where he wanted to work, pure and simple. He had a keen eye and so was not about to do garbage just for the sake of working. But he saw potential in *Flying Home*. He was aware of the director's reputation for quality and, although in hindsight *Flying Home* did seem a bit pat and predictable, it was the opportunity to be the lead in his very first film. As far as acting challenges went, the biggest appeared to be modifying his Irish brogue to a believable American voice. Jamie was also quick to notice how important *The Fall* could ultimately be in his career as it was already paying dividends months before anyone had actually seen it.

What Jamie discovered was that filming Flying Home allowed him the opportunity to stretch as an actor. Along the way he was required to portray a mercenary business man, a good natured manipulator and somebody amazed and forthcoming in life and love. *Flying Home* was a modestly budgeted film, one which Jamie easily gravitated to. His television experience had stepped him in working well and fast and his 'let's do it' attitude quickly made him a favorite of the cast and crew. As fitting a lot of independent films, Flying Home, would not begin to reach a sizeable audience until 2014 but, like The Fall, it kept the word of mouth going. Yes Jamie was that model who, by the way, was one hell of an actor.

Jamie would continue to model on a sporadic basis through 2012. At this point it was simply a matter of keeping his foot in with some by the numbers editorial layouts. The two layouts that jumped out during this period were a Country Casuals spread for *Esquire UK* in which Jamie did his model turns as a clothes horse for the likes of Dior, Homme and Givenchy and a stark bit of bristling series of poses for *Shortlist Mode Magazine*.

At this juncture, Jamie had become the go to model for anti- modeling quotes. But as his acting career had begun to take off, he had tired of seeing mild tirades against the hand that had been feeding him quite well making him out to be a pretentious dick. And so interviewers expecting more of the same from Jamie and at this point were greeted by a more introspective and, yes, polite observer of his modeling life.

"Modeling has been very good to me," he told *Shortlist Mode Magazine*. "I've earned money from it and I've had the opportunity to travel. But that's about it for me. There are not many places you can go in modeling. I've nothing left to achieve in it."

Jamie's brief but impactful stint on *Once Upon A Time* was continuing nearly two years after his last appearance. The emails and texts begging, often fervently, for the return of Sheriff Graham/The Huntsman in some capacity was a constant topic on internet fan pages. The producers took the hint and, in several interviews, teased that everybody involved was trying to work around the actor's busy schedule and bring Jamie back to the fold. For his part, Jamie indicated that he was still in touch with the producers and cast members and that anything was possible.

The Fall had its official unveiling in May 2013 and, by BBC standards, was an unprecedented hit. The ratings were massive and the reviews were fantastic. The show, in general, received rave notices and Jamie in particular was cited for the depth and believability of his acting; good notices that were often couched in backhanded amazement that a model could actually act. In an unprecedented move from the normally conservative BBC 2, The Fall was renewed for a second season by the third episode.

Jamie continued to be grateful at the impact *The Fall* was having on his career. The reality was that *The Fall*'s monstrous word of mouth regarding

Jamie's abilities was continuing to reach out and, by the time of *The Fall*'s airing, he was already on to yet another British TV mini- series… *New Worlds*.

New Worlds actually had its origins in 2008 when a four part historical mini-series called *The Devil's Whore*, which chronicled the life, loves and historical adventure surrounding the English Civil War in the years 1638-1660, was released to good reviews, decent ratings and just as quickly disappeared, seemingly without a trace of recognition. That is until early 2013 when the company that produced *The Devil's Whore* announced that a sequel, entitled New Worlds, would continue the historical saga.

In the follow up, Jamie played the role of medical student Able Goffe who is unexpectedly uprooted from his studies in London, because of the activities of his exiled rebel father, and meets up with a group of idealistic outlaws whose goal is to bring justice to England and to end the tyrannical rule of the Stewart family. Along the way, Able meets up with a girl literally from the other side of the tracks and love ultimately triumphs over all.

Jamie thrived as an actor within the context of this period piece, showcasing a deft hand at different emotions while relishing the abundance of physical action in the storyline. As he offered in *Red Carpet News*, "I personally loved running around the woods with a gun."

"Able seems to run around a lot," Jamie told *WhatsOnTV* while filming the series. "I've got a dodgy shoulder so luckily there hasn't been too much physical fighting. They're a little cautious about letting actors near horses too much. One time, when a horse wasn't behaving during a close up, I ended up riding a stunt man's shoulders."

His work on *New Worlds* was a perfect example of how far Jamie had come in the eyes of casting directors. The days when he was being offered fairly simple takes on his perceived modeling abilities were gone and in their place had been a myriad of different opportunities that played on his talents rather than stereotyping. And nobody was happier with that turn of events than Jamie.

"That's the thing you want most as an actor, a diversity of characters," he explained to *WhatsOnTV*. "It keeps it interesting. I like the challenge of playing different roles. There's always a fear of typecasting. I wouldn't want to do just one thing for the rest of my life. It's nice to mix things up."

And he would, with the first season's filming of The Fall behind him, point with legitimate pride to the fact he had truly brought a monster to life and that, yes, it had been his ultimate acting challenge. "This guy has two young kids," he explained to *Esquire UK*. "He's a good father. But he stalks women at night and strangles them to death.

"To be honest, it was a bit of a headfuck."

It also turned out to be a role that would often, psychologically, drive the actor to darkness and solitude once the day's shooting was over. The nightmares had become a fairly regular occurrence but, when awake, it was not that simple as he explained to *ASOS*. "It was very difficult to be in that headspace. Some nights I had to be alone, take a bath…

"…And think about what I had done."

CHAPTER FIFTEEEN
ONE AND ONE MAKE THREE

Late in January Jamie and Amelia decided to go on holiday.

Jamie was weighing offers at the time but, at the moment was not working, and the couple thought it would be fun to see a bit of the states. Florida proved to be their destination. Given his rapidly rising status as a celebrity, it was not surprising that the paparazzi were all over the couple, especially on a day when they decided on a day at the beach. Jamie looked lean and content as he and Amelia, hot in a tight white bikini, frolicked and hugged in the ocean. One photographer grabbed what many considered the money shot when he captured Amelia's hand sporting a magnificent engagement ring. The relationship between Jamie and Amelia was definitely shaping up as the real thing.

That Jamie was happy did not, to that point, result in overly effusive comments about the love of his life. Short and clipped was pretty much the order of the day when, in *British Vogue*, he related of Amelia "She's dream stuff. She's amazing."

And what many did not realize was that by the end of April, she would become Mrs. Jamie Dornan.

The happy couple were fairly discreet with their wedding plans, reportedly announcing their big day only a matter of days before the ceremony took place and then, almost matter of factly in some well-placed texts. Those on the invite list had played along with the clandestine nature of their plans and the press was pretty much threadbare when it came to any reported particulars.

A week before they would be married, Jamie was in a state of emotional bliss that he had never encountered before. So much so that he would reveal in *The Sunday Times* how he had spent a recent night alone, writing his wedding vows and finally bursting into tears at the turn his life was about to take. He had the woman of his dreams and a career that was definitely on the rise. As he spoke with *The Sunday Times*, he agreed with the idea that, in the finest tradition of 'and they lived happily ever after', he seemed to have it all.

"I hope so," he said. "I want to have all that. I'd say I'm pretty ready. I want to experience it while I'm still young."

On April 27, 2013, Jamie and Amelia exchanged marriage vows in front of assembled family and friends at a beautiful country house in Somerset, England. Great pains had been taken to keep the ceremony low key and the result was that the event, by all accounts, had been paparazzi free. Jamie had continued to keep close ties with his former cast mates from *Once Upon A Time*, with Giniffer Goodwin, Josh Dallas and Jennifer Morrison in attendance among the well-wishers.

Jamie was basking in the emotional high that

signaled the next phase of his life. He reflected on that day in conversation with *ASOS* when he said, "It's an important day. All the people you love are there to watch you have a brilliant day."

Jamie, in the meantime, had accepted the starring role in *New Worlds* and by May was on the set filming. Amelia reportedly spent time with him while he was filming and when they were apart, they were constantly texting and phoning. Amelia, true to her acting background, understood that *New Worlds* was something Jamie could not pass on. But the newly married couple were united in the fact that Jamie's latest career step would just have to wait. Because Jamie and Amelia already had their honeymoon all planned out.

Immediately after they said their 'I do's,' the couple hopped a plane for the US. They landed on the east coast where they commandeered a classic convertible Mustang and began a leisurely five week drive across the United States. Amelia had never learned to drive and so it was left up to Jamie to be at the wheel for the entire six thousand mile odyssey. As fate would have it, *The Fall* would premiere during their honeymoon road trip. As Jamie laughingly explained to *The Journal*, they were operating in a literal vacuum when it came to friends and family.

"No one likes to bother you when you're on your honeymoon. But I was thinking the show's been on for 30 seconds and no one's been in touch yet."

After a fun loving excursion, during which Jamie told *The Journal* they had indulged in "a lot of drinking, table tennis and just bumming around", Jamie and Amelia ended up in Los Angeles for a last round of sightseeing before catching a flight back to London.

Seven weeks after the ceremony, the happy couple announced that Amelia was pregnant.

On a low-key trip back to Jamie's hometown, Holywood, a wellbeing scan was conducted by Jamie's stepmother, Samina Dornan, at the Lisbun Roads healthcare clinic. It was Samina who broke the news to *The Belfast Telegraph*. "The early wellbeing scanning was a beautiful and emotional experience for all present." She would later confirm the blessed event when she told *The Sunday Life*, "Jim and I are delighted that our third grandchild is on the way."

Those inclined to do the math and working back from her due date could have easily speculated that Amelia was already pregnant before they tied the knot. In fact *The Belfast Telegraph* hinted as much when it reported that Amelia had been spotted drinking only water during a romantic meal around the time of the wedding.

But even the ever probing tabloid press had seemed inclined to steer clear of even this minor bit of scandal. It was as if Jamie and Amelia had emerged as the consummate fairy tale couple, impervious to any controversy. It was as if the world had decided to be less cynical for a time and revel in what they perceived as a happy ending.

Through the summer, Jamie was of two minds. He was quite at ease with being a husband and, soon, a father. He was enjoying the simple outings and errands in London and even seemed at ease that the paparazzi were back and snapping away.

That he had also been working on *New Worlds*

during the early stages of Amelia's pregnancy also gave him a sense of well-being as he offered to *TV Times*. "I have a pregnant wife at home at the moment so I really wanted to stay in the UK. That just seemed to make sense to me."

But it was not long after the premiere of *The Fall* that Jamie discovered his serial killer/family man had become an immediate pop culture sensation. And whereas before he could move about the streets in relative anonymity, he was now a well- known television star and with stardom came the attention.

He recalled in a conversation with reporter Megan Mackay that appeared in *Red Carpet News* how even a simple jaunt downtown had suddenly turned into chaos at his very presence. "I was on the tube and all of a sudden somebody shouted 'There's the serial killer' and people started to panic and stare at me."

And the tube incident was only the beginning.

"I began being recognized on the street as Spector," Jamie told *The Journal*. "People would say things like 'There's the serial killer!' It's not a reaction you really need."

But it was a backhanded acknowledgement that Jamie was quite the actor.

While he was enjoying his time as a newlywed and expectant father, the adrenaline junkie in Jamie was also anxious for the next step in his career. Which came with the announcement that he was being put up for the role of Christian Grey in the film adaptation of *Fifty Shades of Grey*. When he did not get it, he was philosophical about it all.

But then fate stepped in. For whatever reason,

and over the ensuing weeks there would be quite a few, Charlie Hunnam suddenly backed out of the project. Before he knew it Jamie was quite literally whisked off the set of *New Worlds* and on a red eye flight to Los Angeles where he once again auditioned with Dakota Johnson. The conversations and auditions were quick and to the point. No punches were pulled and no attempts were made to sugarcoat for the sake of an actor's ego. Jamie knew he was the second choice if he got the role and he was fine with that.

"I already got a glimpse of working with Sam at the test and I had met Dakota by then," he told *The London Evening Standard*. "So I had an idea of how it would be if I got the part."

Then it was back to London where he would sit and wait for the phone to ring. It did and the role of Christian Grey was now officially his.

But first there was that simple matter of breaking the news to his very pregnant, raging with hormones wife that he was about to star in the film version of the most erotically and sexually charged books on the literary scene and that he would most likely be filmed in the kind of altogether that would make his photo sessions for Calvin Klein seem PG by comparison.

Shortly after he put down the phone that early morning in late October, Amelia was up and he was about to break the news to her. He was adamant in talking to *Shortlist* that the decision on whether or not he took the role was pretty much in her hands.

"A lot of people would have had a shit fit at thirty something weeks pregnant, hearing, 'Darling we're going to Vancouver this week for four months. We're going to have a Canadian baby and I'm doing a film where, for parts of it, I will be naked.' That was a tough pitch...

...Fortunately my wife is a brilliant, understanding person."

Two weeks after being selected to play Christian Grey, Jamie ended a long isolation from the *Twitterverse* when he logged in for the first time. Most were expecting the first of many reports on all things Fifty Shades as it pertained to his character. But, according to the *International Business Times*, what they got instead was effusive praise for a recently run commercial for a Belfast jewelry store called Fred J. Malcolm Ltd. According to the story, Malcolm, a long-time family friend, had off handedly suggested that Jamie might be the perfect person to play the young man in the commercial who is trying to find the perfect way and jewelry to tell the love of his life he wanted to marry her. Jamie, according to a tweet by Malcolm, had equally off handedly agreed to do it but then he got busy.

After that original tweet, Jamie quickly warmed to the idea of letting the world know what was going on with him. He was quick to get the hang of things and was soon tweeting and texting like a fiend. And yet another aspect of his life suddenly changed...

...Forever.

CHAPTER SIXTEEN
WALK LIKE A GREY

Jamie's selection to play Christian Grey caught a lot of people by surprise.

A few industry insiders were aware of Jamie, more from his modeling credentials than his admittedly slim acting resume. And never far from their thoughts was the old saw that models can't act And so there were shockwaves and, much like what had transpired with Dakota Johnson, a certain degree of fan backlash. However once the dust settled and the world got around to the fact that Jamie would, indeed, be playing the most kinky billionaire, the hoopla died down and the press got down to the business of letting rabid fans know who this mysterious Jamie Dornan was.

For his part, Jamie seemed alternately bemused and amazed at the passion generated by his being chosen to play Christian. "I am never going to please all 100 million people," he told *The Independent*. "I know there are campaigns of hate against me already."

Jamie was quite accommodating in those early days of the press rush, answering questions both probing and trivial. Having gone through this routine for years with the fashion press, he was actually quite comfortable and articulate in his home spun Irish way. Once the press got past the expected, and quite extended bio questions, they would invariably focus on the business at hand, Christian Grey and how he plans to play him. It was with those questions that Jamie's character and personality shined through.

"I'm not afraid to play Christian Grey," he told *Glamour Poland*. "I'm not like him but I perfectly understand him. I never thought of him as a monster. He is simply someone who is woven from his desires."

In the same conversation, Jamie indicated that anyone expecting a method type performance from him would be sadly disappointed. "I don't have an acting strategy. There is a distinct lack of method in how I approach things. I go in, say my lines, go home and read a book. I don't understand people who do not read."

Finally Jamie had a tongue in cheek response when *Glamour Poland* suggested that the role of Christian would play into the sexual fantasies of literally millions of women. "I would hope that after playing Christian, women will see me as a real guy."

Simply being selected to play the iconic and kinky Christian Grey in the most anticipated film in eons was the easy part for Jamie. What he had only partially anticipated was the mountains of paperwork and red tape that went hand in hand with his talent.

As well as some physical alterations to his appearance. Ever since he began modeling, Jamie, quite naturally, had taken to wearing facial hair. It had improved his luck with the ladies as well as helped him stand out from the often metrosexual modeling crowd. Needless to say he had become quite comfortable with a beard. Sadly one of the first things he was told upon capturing the role of Christian in *Fifty Shades of Grey* was that his character, as described by James in her books, did not have facial hair. And so for the first time in years, Jamie was forced to shave.

"I feel uncomfortable without it," he told *The Guardian*. "I find myself moving differently. I don't like myself without a beard."

Reportedly Jamie was being paid an estimated $1.6 million to do the film. Again that was a pretty straightforward negotiation, take it or leave it. Needless to say Jamie took it. But there were other I's that needed to be dotted and T's to be crossed. And one of the most anticipated was just how much of Jamie audiences would actually see. There had been a long simmering debate among studio executives about the merits of an R-rated vs Unrated film. Economics ultimately dictated an R-rated release but there was still talk about an X-rated version that would show quite a bit of flesh, especially Jamie's.

Jamie, given his Calvin Klein days, could hardly be considered a prude but in several interviews with the likes of *The Guardian* and *The Observer* he addressed the question of his penis in a cool, logical manner. "There were contracts in place saying that the audience would not be seeing my penis. You want to appeal to as wide an audience as possible without grossing them out."

Getting physically inside the character of Christian Grey as depicted by E.L. James in her books was equally challenging to the actor according to a conversation with Interview. "Christian is someone who is careful to keep himself in shape and who spends obscene amounts of money on presenting himself."

The former would not present much of a problem as Jamie was nothing if not compulsive in keeping his body in tip top physical condition. Walking around comfortably in high style suits, on the other hand, was something that took Jamie a while to get used to. "I'm quite awkward in a suit because I don't have the opportunity to wear one very often. But seeing as how Christian wears a suit in roughly eighty percent of the script, I knew that I could learn to be comfortable," he told *Interview.*

One trait that Jamie was having trouble with as he prepared to make the trip to Vancouver to start work on *Fifty Shades of Grey* was the idea of walking with the self-confident air of a self-made man of the world. In that area, Jamie was sorely lacking and the problem had been with him nearly all his life. From an early age, Jamie had developed the habit of walking on his toes. They result was that when he walked there was a distinctive bounce, rather than a strong stride, to his step. The habit had long been a topic of some teasing by his close friends and, while he never gave it much concern, he did admit on *The Graham Norton Show* that, "I've always had a complex with the way I walk."

During the course of their relationship, Amelia had come to notice Jamie's 'bounce' in his step and attempted to help him work through the issue. She suggested that he try leaning back as he walked and she was with him on many days when he would practice walking on the streets of London. But despite

Amelia's efforts, the bounce remained in her lover's step.

Fifty Shades director Sam Taylor Johnson was not the first professional to point out that Jamie had a certain spring to his step. The director of *The Fall* had noticed Jamie's unorthodox gait and had asked Jamie if that was his own walk or if it was an improvisational walk he was doing for the role. When Jamie confessed that the walk was all his, the director suggested that he take longer strides. It was a help but it was not a cure.

Jamie arrived in Vancouver in early November, some days before the production would be officially up and running. When the film would start and when Fifty Shades would be released had been changed several times. The best Jamie could fathom at that point was that the movie would begin production December 1. But before then, there was some personal business that needed his attention. Amelia, now in the final weeks of her pregnancy, would be joining him shortly in Vancouver and so the first order of business was to rent a home close by where *Fifty Shades* would be filming. Jamie was mentally at all ends, the particulars of the film and what it would do for his career and the prospects of becoming a father. Needless to say the later was running slightly ahead of the former.

"I don't think there's anything negative about being a dad," he offered to *Notebook*. "I basically had no idea what to expect."

Arriving in Vancouver early also gave him an opportunity to get the lay of the land and to work on a couple of other issues necessary to his building the perfect Christian Grey. Jamie would be the first to admit that he was only an adequate dancer at best and a sequence in the film would require him to perform the perfect Foxtrot with Anastasia. The production had brought in a dance instructor to mentor Jamie on the fine art of the dance.

"It was the Foxtrot," Jamie told Graham Norton. "It was a very classic kind of dance and I was struggling with it. Finally the teacher said 'you know what you need to do is think about dancing as walking, you need to think about it in terms of walking heel to toe.' "

Jamie thought about the correlation for a bit and it seemed to make perfect sense, especially as he felt it related to his issue with walking. "No one ever told me that," he related to Graham Norton. "Now I apply that every day when I'm walking around."

The upshot was that Jamie did learn the Foxtrot and had made great strides in being able to walk like a Grey.

Jamie was never what you would consider a method actor, *The Fall* providing ample evidence as to how he could turn a character on and off as needed. But when it came to getting to the nitty gritty of Christian Grey and his rather kinky proclivities, he felt he needed to go to the source and, on his own, hired a S&M expert to show him the ropes (no pun intended). "It was such a big part of my character that I wanted to know what I was doing," he told *Shortlist*. "So this guy and his submissive come over

and showed me how things were done.

"I sat in the corner of the room with a beer and just watched. My driver was waiting on the other side of the door. I don't know what he was thinking."

In an interview with *Elle UK,* and later reported by *The Wrap* and other outlets, Jamie had a good laugh at the experience, relating that he good naturedly exhorted the performers to really give him a show and he did concede that he saw "plenty of kink" during the session and that he found the experience "interesting." So much so that he took one precaution before going home to be with his wife and child.

"I felt I needed to take a long shower before I touched either one of them."

CHAPTER SEVENTEEN
FIRST DAYS ON FIFTY

Fifty Shades of Grey was finally confirmed to start filming on December 1, 2013. In late November, Amelia went into labor and would deliver a healthy baby girl. No name or details of the birth were forthcoming and so the tabloid and gossip press ran with the scraps, which included speculation that the baby had been born in either Canada, the US or the UK.

The reality was that Jamie was over the moon about being a new father. "I love fatherhood," he told *The Telegraph*. "That's a new challenge and adventure. You might sleep a bit less but you've got this small life to look after."

Consequently it was a very fatigued but deliriously happy Jamie who reported to the downtown Vancouver set of *Fifty Shades of Grey* on Day One. Not surprisingly, the normally crowded and chaotic tourist area of Gas Town was even more so as an estimated 200 cast and crew members descended on the area and began putting up their lights and equipment. In an attempt to put off an anticipated and disruptive rush of paparazzi and Fifty fanatics, the production was going under the code name of *The Adventures of Max and Banks*. However based on the crowds that swarmed the area on that first day, the code name fooled absolutely nobody. *Fifty Shades* author E.L. James was on hand for the occasion, texting and instagraming away. Finally at the appointed moment, director Sam Taylor Young yelled action and the *Fifty Shades of Grey* train officially left the station.

Those anticipating an immediate jump into hot sex scenes were, doubtless, disappointed as the big sequence of the day was Christian quizzing Anastasia about her dating and family life while drinking tea in an outdoor café. Jamie seemed at ease in his first shot, projecting the quiet cool of Christian as he played on Anastasia's innocence. In fact, while most set reports of that day indicated a palpable level of nerves and anticipation, all were quick to point out that the chemistry between Jamie and Dakota was quite good and, more importantly to the camera's lens, believable.

The production was well aware of Jamie and his wife's blessed event and while *Fifty Shades of Grey* was definitely on a schedule that had to be met, they were more than willing to juggle that schedule so that scenes telling how Anastasia came to meet Christian, and would not require Jamie, could be shot, giving the actor a much appreciated couple of days to be home with his wife and to bond with his newborn daughter.

Jamie reportedly had made an easy transition from actor to father. He was constantly available to the needs of his wife and newborn daughter, proving quite adept at pitching in when a diaper needed to be changed and often up first to check on his daughter's midnight cries so that Amelia could get much needed sleep.

The time away would also give the public relations spinners on the film an opportunity to deflect the inevitable rumors of discord that had begun to pop up. One story in particular had tension brewing between the director and *Fifty Shades* author over the direction the script was taking. A rumor quickly squelched when an Instagram photo of Johnson and James in a mocking good natured punch up.

When it came to the on- set relationship between Dakota and Jamie, no spin seemed necessary. They immediately bonded around the fact that they were both still relative newcomers on the scene and appeared cut from the same laidback attitudes. In between shots they would often be found hanging out together, sometimes joking and laughing easily and sometimes not saying much but just hanging out together. The last thing *Fifty Shades* needed was a clash of egos and diva attitudes. And that, fortunately, was the last thing they seemed to be getting.

Jamie returned to the *Fifty Shades* set. In the back of his mind had to be the question of when the filming would take the turn everybody expected. The stuff that had made the books international bestsellers. The sex.

What Jamie had quickly discovered was that director Sam Taylor Johnson was building on a notion of romance as well as seduction and so the scenes that Jamie returned to were relationship moments caught in time rather than a quick run up to the erotic moments. And in a sense Jamie was thankful that many of those early scenes, such as Christian's attendance at

Anastasia's graduation and his meeting her parents for the first time, were layering on subtle character in which Jamie was given the opportunity to exercise confidence and a rising sense of control.

That Johnson was wielding a strong directorial hand was helpful in those moments where Jamie seemed tentative. And when Johnson was not available to set things right in one particular scene, it remained for actor Victor Rasuk to literally push Jamie in the right direction.

"There's a scene where he [Christian] pushes me," Rasuk told *Watch*. "I remember the first few takes and Jamie was pushing me very lightly. When it was suggested that he push me a bit harder, he was like 'Hey man, can I really push you that hard?' I said, 'Dude of course. I've been working out.' So on the next take he pushes me so hard that I almost fall on my ass."

The early days of filming also gave Jamie's Christian an opportunity to showcase a light romantic touch as in the scenes in which Dakota and Christian are walking light and carefree down a city street and breaking into an impromptu ballroom dance amid the crowds around them.

When not filming, the difference between Jamie and Dakota's respective lifestyles was much in evidence. Dakota would be out seeing the sights or shopping with friends. On the other hand, Jamie could not get home fast enough to be with his family in private moments.

No one could doubt that Jamie was not taking *Fifty Shades of Grey* seriously. He was the first one to approach the director if he had a question or suggestion. He was always on time, no matter how little sleep he had the night before, and he knew his lines. Which was not to say that Dakota was not equally dedicated. But it would turn out that a difference in attitude between the two actors would eventually raise some red flags.

Quite simply Dakota was nice to a fault. And quick to point out in AsiaOne.com that the second choice to play Christian had been the right one. "Ultimately the decision that was made was great," she said. "Jamie's wonderful. I'm really excited for people to see him." And while being nice to the press was one thing, potentially disrupting the film's shooting schedule was quite another.

Anybody who happened to cross Dakota's path was immediately up for a good morning, how's the family and the latest gossip. There was nothing deliberate in the way she interacted with crew members, security, other actors, fans and even the odd paparazzi who happened to cross her path. This was just Dakota being her natural outgoing self.

By contrast, Jamie was solitary and private by nature and, when not working, would often be off to his trailer or standing alone in a secluded part of the filming location. It soon became evident that those contrasting styles would often by a loggerheads.

When Dakota was being social she tended to get easily distracted from the business at hand. And being on a fairly tight schedule, those little moments of delay could easily add up. Jamie soon became aware of the problem and took it upon himself to intercede. Several reports from the set during those early days of filming alleged that Jamie, on several occasions, had walked up to Dakota when he sensed that the conversation she was engaged in had gone on too long and, rather sternly, had told the other person that Dakota needed to be left alone. Was this Jamie channeling Christian as part of his acting approach or was there something in his overprotective nature that had suddenly moved to the fore? It remained to be seen.

However there was more than enough evidence to contrast the notion that Jamie was a self-absorbed hermit on the set. Reports emanating from *Fifty Shades* indicated that Jamie's subtle, self- effacing humor was a hit with the cast and crew and that he was, given the right moment, an animated conversationalist. It was also reported that many a break from filming found the assembled cast and crew being entertained by Jamie singing soft Irish songs.

One element of Jamie's nature that seemed to soften during the making of the film was his dealings with the paparazzi. After spending years railing against the renegade photographers, Jamie soon found himself once again put to the test on the occasions when the family would venture out on Vancouver's streets for a bit of fresh air. An unwritten rule among the paparazzi was to be delicate in approaching him and, especially his wife and daughter. Keep a respectable distance, take a requisite number of snaps and then leave. As long as they followed those rules, Jamie seemed at ease with the intrusion and there were no reports of angry confrontations during his stay in Vancouver.

A big part of Jamie's comfort in Vancouver was that the vibe on the set of *Fifty Shades of Grey* continued to be very family friendly. It was not

Inside Grey's Anatomy: The Unauthorized Biography of Jamie Dornan

uncommon for Amelia and the baby to visit the set while Jamie was working. But, as reported by various media outlets, it was only during what were considered the more sedate scenes. Perhaps it was just coincidence or that Jamie and Amelia had established certain ground rules. But for whatever reason, when Jamie was to be involved in anything involving romance or more, Amelia was conspicuous by her absence.

The film would remain on schedule and on budget, the numerous supporting actors would come and go with precision and professionalism. Which is why the producers felt comfortable knocking off a few days before Christmas. For Jamie and family it was a joyous holiday. A good-sized tree was brought into their rental home. Jamie was the doting dad and loving husband according to those who were around the couple during Christmas. Vancouver in December. For Jamie, it was most certainly his joyous refuge.

Vancouver hit a bad patch of weather in the post-Christmas season and it was at that point, according to a *Digital Journal* story, that *Fifty Shades* temporarily left for the warmer climes of Tenerife in the Canary Islands to shoot some scenes involving Christian's business side as well as the much speculated upon honeymoon sequence. This was also the sign post of *Fifty Shades* was finally heading off into erotic territory.

Speculation had become the watchword with the *Fifty Shades of Grey* production. The latest round of rumors centering around the fact that the studio was getting cold feet about the possibilities of Fifty Shades as a successful trilogy of films and was thinking seriously about condensing all three books into one film. Another story suggested that much of the scenes being shot in Tenerife were actually scenes from the third book.

All Jamie knew was that he was about to shoot the meat of the whole *Fifty Shades* phenomena. So to speak.

CHAPTER EIGHTEEN
SEX: ISN'T IT ROMANTIC?

"Mmm. He's soft and hard all at once. Like steel encased in velvet. Surprisingly tasty, salty and smooth."

This line from the novel *Fifty Shades of Grey* is a lot for any actor to aspire to, let alone succeed as the ultimate sex mate Christian Grey. But to here screenwriter Kelly Marcel describe it in an episode of *An Evening In The Writer's Room*, Jamie definitely climbed that *Fifty Shades* mountain.

"Jamie is great at being soft and hard," joshed Marcel "which is hard for an actor. He should get an Oscar of some sorts for his sexual performance in this film."

From the moment he landed the role of Christian, Jamie knew he would be bombarded with questions and intrusive speculation regarding the erotic moments in *Fifty Shades of Grey*. And it was to his credit that, with the complete support of his wife and family, he was comfortable in talking about the things that everybody wanted to talk about, such as ropes, blindfolds and all manner of S&M regalia as well as how he comported himself in the film's sexually charged world. And as he explained in Entertainment Weekly, he was at ease in this world.

"I'm a fairly worldly guy," he offered. "I grew up in a fairly liberal place. I'm not saying we had a playroom but I'm not shocked by the sex in the book. It's essential to telling the story."

He also knew well before the first take of the first scene that the key to making a believably erotic story was good chemistry between Dakota and himself. And he knew that they were both on sturdy ground in that regard before filming began. "We had an undeniable chemistry while doing those scenes," he said in an interview with Today. "Having trust was a big part of it."

Early snippets of the more erotic moments from the film had been edited to make them viewable on more family friendly talk shows. But enough of the erotic clinches and S&M moments have aired to make it plain that both actors were definitely into the moment. Or so it seemed.

Dakota had been quick to burst the bubble when she explained, in a *Today* interview that "The sex was mechanical. It was more like a task."

Jamie joined in that tone by citing, in The Observer, that no he did not get turned on during the scene in which he spanks Anastasia. "Anyone who thinks that actors get turned on by doing a sex scene in a film is mistaken. There are dozens of hairy men standing around moving cables and lighting equipment. That's not sexy unless you get turned on by having people watch. Which I'm not."

As Jamie patently trudged through the seemingly endless rounds of sex questions, it became evident that the interviewers were looking for something outrageous rather than logical in his answers. But Jamie ultimately stood by the fact that even the most sexual of moments were simply a job that he was being paid quite handsomely to do.

"What can I say except that it's all very choreographed and very much like sexual acrobatics," he told Today. "The reality of it is that is that there's like this burly man you don't know very well, who is three feet away from your face, filming you. Which is usually not the way that most people have sex. Not me anyway."

In the media blitz that had dogged *Fifty Shades of Grey* throughout the production to this point, much was made of the fact that the filmmakers were creating a sexual environment that might be misinterpreted by filmgoers and critics. Jamie had gotten to the point where he had heard it all before and told The Guardian that the sexuality in the movie was literally by the book.

"I think it's very hard to argue that the sex in the movie is not all consensual," he said. "Half the book is about making contracts, getting permissions and agreements that have to be made. There is no rape and there are no forced sexual situations."

Jamie would often acknowledge that he had full confidence in the director to set the right tone for the more torrid scenes. He indicated that she was coming from a unique perspective that would most certainly work to the betterment of the film. But he would be candid in a *Daily Mail* story on how he would not be certain of how the sex was ultimately being handled until he saw the final cut of the film.

"There might be some suggestive elements but I haven't seen it at this stage. So it's hard for me to say. I'm aware of what we shot and it wasn't as if we shot a film without any action."

CHAPTER NINETEEN
FALLOUT

Fifty Shades continued production in a workmanlike fashion into January 2014. And, by association, Jamie had become quite familiar with the routine of filming. The increased instance of the various components of the sex scenes was always cause for a bit of normal tension on the set but the chemistry and acting shorthand that came with familiarity had served Jamie and his co-star well. Jamie was dealing with it in a quite matter of fact manner.

Not that Jamie was not aware of the worldwide interest and speculation that was following his and the movie's every turn. On more than one occasion, and he acknowledged probably against his better judgment, he had pursued the blogosphere and was well aware that there was still a faction of haters who, even at this juncture, felt he was not right for the part of Christian. He was well aware of the expectations and the pressures of *Fifty Shades* being a huge success rather than a legendary failure right up there with *Heaven's Gate* and *Ishtar*. But, as he explained on *The Graham Norton Show*, all of that was pretty much out of his hands at this point.

"We're in a very powerful position," he offered. "Ninety plus million people have read the book. If a third of that number see the film, it will be a nice position to be in. But I have no idea ultimately what the film is going to do."

Reports of Jamie's capabilities and a kinky, and quite menacing, Christian Grey were very good for Jamie, in a way. However when coupled with the raves he had already received as serial killer Paul Spector in *The Fall*, and with a second season of The Fall scheduled to go into production soon, Jamie was already reading media speculation that he had already been typecast by Hollywood as the go to sociopath and psycho. Jamie acknowledged that possibility but seemed determined to avoid typecasting at all costs.

"It does make you slightly conscious," he said in an aside to *Huffington Post UK*. "No actor wants to be typecast. You want to be clever and pick things that show you're not just a one trick pony. Besides, I just don't know how many sexy sociopath roles there are available to be typecast."

It remained that the ultimate sexy sociopath, Christian Grey was, by this time very much in his acting wheelhouse as the last weeks of *Fifty Shades of Grey* wound down in Vancouver. Jamie reportedly had evolved so naturally into the guise of Christian that it was only when he would break into a smile or joke in between scenes that people knew it was truly Jamie and that he was merely playing a character.

The Fifty Shades of Grey production officially brought down the curtain on February 23, 2014 when the final scene under director Johnson's practiced eye came to a conclusion and the director, all smiles and yes exhaustion, most likely yelled 'cut. Print it' to shouts and applause from the cast and crew. E.L. James, who had been on set several times during the production, was on hand for the occasion, made the conclusion of filming official to the world when she snapped an Instagram photo of director Johnson and herself holding up what appeared to be glasses of champagne. Underneath the photo was a caption that announced, 'That's a wrap.'

Jamie did not waste any time. After making his goodbyes, Jamie quickly packed up his family and belongings and was soon on a plane back to the UK where he immediately set up residence once again in London and reacquainted himself with British time. But, figuratively and literally, by the time he was once again home, he was already being seen as Christian Grey only weeks after the conclusion of filming.

The studio, perhaps bowing to the demand to see something of the just completed film, made an unannounced appearance in March at the Las Vegas Cinema Con, bearing some very rough but reportedly enticing footage of Jamie and Dakota that would be the first look for those who happened to be there. Reportedly the leaked footage emphasized the romance and seduction aspects of the movie with little if any hints of the expected eroticism. The response was excitement of the moment to those privy to the sneak peak and Jamie on screen looked very much what millions of fans had hoped to see in Christian.

Jamie did not have time to consider the ramifications of this sneak peak. He was already back on the second season of The Fall and his favorite alter ego Paul Spector. While still doing *Fifty Shades of*

Grey, Jamie had received an episode by episode breakdown of where the second season would take his character. And as he would explain to the *Herts & Essex Observer*, "I was genuinely shaking. I was so excited."

The reason being that Season 2 of *The Fall*, while continuing the emotional and psychological template of the previous episodes, was staking out even a more expansive territory. With a storyline that begins approximately ten days after the first season climax, we find Spector, family in tow, on the run and hiding out in Scotland with the equally fractured police detective Stella Gibson in hot pursuit. Jamie was appreciative that Season 2 would be filmed on location in Scotland after *Fifty Shades* had taken him around the world. But more importantly, the actor in him, was thankful that, creatively, Spector was going places.

"There's a slightly different tone with the second series," he told *Herts & Essex Observer*. "The first series was more about the act of killing while the second is about what activates the act and the hunt."

Jamie would acknowledge that his current state as a family man had immediately given him new insights into the duplicity of Spector and would make him much more believable in the character. On the other hand, he would spend many nights with a slight shiver as he digested the dichotomy of his real world and that of the serial killer he was playing.

"I like playing characters that are fractured and broken," he explored in *Digital Spy*. "I find those characters more relatable for some reason. "I don't feel like I'm like that by nature."

The only stumbling block for Jamie was fatigue. *The Fall* was scheduled to start filming literally one day after filming on *Fifty Shades of Grey* concluded. Jamie had admitted in *Digital Spy* that he had essentially had one week of rest and that he was bordering on exhaustion. He was thankful that the show's creator, and now fulltime director, Allan Cubitt had reconfigured the schedule to fit Jamie's life situation that would finally push the start date to mid-March.

"My goal was to make sure I was there," he said. "I found myself very eager to become Paul Spector again."

March 2014 would be the beginning of Jamie's official coronation as a rising star. In March he would capture best actor for *The Fall* from the Broadcasting Press Guild. In April the Irish Film and Television Awards would bestow Jamie with twin honors for *The Fall*, Best Lead Actor in Television and Rising Star. Jamie, who had been a presenter at the IFTA awards the previous year, explained to *Red Carpet News* that he had promised himself that he would not return if he was not nominated. "It's nice to be recognized in that way," he said. "Life is good at the moment."

And finally, in May, he would receive a nomination for Best Lead Actor from the British Academy Television Awards. Interviewed by *GQ UK* after the ceremonies, and with Amelia looking radiant at his side, Jamie was basking in the limelight when he said "It was lovely to be nominated but, to be honest, once you get there, you want to win. I'm a competitive little bastard."

Jamie had little time to savor the honors as, by

that time, he was back to work on *The Fall*.

It was literally old home week when Jamie and the production convened in Scotland. Anderson and the other cast members and crew had been on to other things since the first season and so there were endless lives and stories to catch up on. Jamie was quite familiar with the Scottish landscape and easily picked out favorite haunts amid the show's locations.

"It's lovely being home with family and friends," he told a pool of reporters visiting *The Fall* set. "This job feels like coming home."

But it was coming home to a different atmosphere. Jamie's worldwide notoriety as the star of *Fifty Shades of Grey*, suddenly had cast and crew looking at the actor in a way that played to the fantasy. Before he had been just Jamie. However now, especially in the eyes of the women in the production, he was their very own sex symbol. No less a light than his co-star Gillian Anderson had a good laugh at the sexual tension on the set in a conversation with BBC. "I could only see him naked from the moment he walked in. It was really distracting."

By this time, the mania for Jamie as Spector was running a fairly close second to his notoriety as Christian and so the press were swarming throughout the production of what would ultimately be an 11 episode season. Jamie had become quite good at dropping tantalizing teases to interviewers while not giving anything away and so quotes about 'things about this season surprising even me' and 'we're going to see a different side of Spector' were delivered with equal parts sincerity and public relations hucksterism to generate maximum media interest.

One quip that made quite a bit of news was the response to the question of how long he expected the series to go? Jamie matter of factly acknowledged that a third season of *The Fall* might well take a different turn and that his character might not be around for a third season.

But by the time *The Fall* wrapped its second season, Jamie was already of a state of mind to keep the career ball rolling. Not that he was looking for a reason to be away from his wife and daughter. When with his family, he was totally the loving husband, the doting father and all sorts of happy with his life as it now stood. However, and with a totally understanding, supportive and encouraging Amelia at his side, Jamie was well aware that he needed to keep working for his family and for himself.

"The operative word is 'working' he told a group of reporters including *Digital Spy*. "That's the thing that you want to keep doing. I guess I'm just happy for the work."

And much like his co-star Dakota, good word of mouth emanating from the *Fifty Shades of Grey* movie had immediately put Jamie at the top of the casting list for several in development projects that would most certainly keep the actor busy throughout the coming year.

First out of the chute will be *Adam Jones* (aka *The Chef*) which stars Bradley Cooper, Uma Thurman and Sienna Miller in a comedy centered around a chef who pulls together a crew to create the ultimate restaurant.

The 9th Life of Louis Drax will showcase Jamie in a psychological/fantasy-tinged thriller in which the actor plays a psychologist who stumbles on an unexpected mystery while treating a boy who survived a near fatal fall.

And finally the period action film *The Siege of Jadotville* in which Jamie portrays Commander Pat Quinlan in a true story of a siege of 150 Irish troopers in the Congo in 1961. In a conversation with *Sunday World*, Jamie appeared particularly keen about this film. "I can't wait to get stuck in *Jadotville*. It's an unbelievable story and Commander Pat Quinlan is going to be a treat of a character to tackle."

In the case of *Jadotville*, it appears that signing Jamie to the role may have been the main reason that the film was being made. The script had been kicking around for some time and according to director Ritchie Smyth, who praised Jamie's performance in *The Fall* to *Sunday World*, "Jamie has been instrumental in bringing this film to life."

Jamie's choices for post *Fifty Shades of Grey* work seemed to be running contrary to the notion of being the hot new kid on the scene. In most cases actors who spring seemingly unknown into the public's consciousness tend to jump right into a big commercial film, a summer blockbuster or a sequel to an established franchise in an attempt to quickly cash in on their sudden notoriety. With Jamie, that was not the case.

He was seemingly choosing projects of a more individual nature rather than a commercial slam dunk, films and parts that would test and showcase his acting ability. To be sure, all of these post *Fifty* films had degrees of commercial possibilities to them but, owing to the vagaries of the film business, none necessarily had massive box office in their future. But on the other side, there was the reality that Jamie in any film would most certainly put fannies in the seats.

Jamie was grateful for the abundance of opportunities in the wake of *Fifty Shades of Grey* and *The Fall*. But in conversation with *GQ UK*, it was evident that at some point he would be in need of some time off.

"I'm very happy but, you know, it's tiring. I feel like I'm aging rapidly."

CHAPTER TWENTY
RESHOOT

Going into October, Jamie was pretty much a homebody and enjoying every bit of it.

With three films in active development it was a safe bet that he would be extremely busy throughout 1015. There was also the television premiere of the second season of *The Fall* set to begin in November and the inherent press obligations to consider. And with *Fifty Shades of Grey* still scheduled for a Valentine's Day 2015 unveiling, Jamie had been warned that promotion and publicity would take up much of late December and all of January. But beyond that actual real acting work on the film had long been regulated some months to the rear.

Or so he thought.

Behind the scenes, and depending on which story you believed, there were problems with the film. The initial cut of *Fifty Shades of Grey* clocked in at a reported 1.57 minutes. The running time was perfect for theater owners in search of maximum showings in a day. But purists balked at the notion that the original story could be told in so short a length without losing structure and content. Particularly concerned was author James who indicated that the film needed more scenes, especially in the area of building the relationship leading up to the expected bedroom antics. At the end of the day, the filmmakers had to agree.

And so in early October Jamie, along with Amelia and their daughter, once again hopped a plane in the UK for a flight to Los Angeles and from there to Vancouver where a series of reshoots were scheduled. Reshoots are not uncommon in filmmaking. Reshoots mere months before the actual release of a film are and, not surprisingly, quickly gave rise to media frenzy of trouble in paradise.

The tabloid and gossip press immediately jumped to the conclusion that the reshoots had been necessary because the chemistry between the two actors had been so bad. Most of the brickbats had been aimed at the lack of personality and passion shown by Dakota, with descriptions like 'naïve' and 'dishrag' being tossed around. But a good number of doubters also had their sights set on Jamie as well, with his attackers sighting weak interaction and just plain bad chemistry between the two actors.

If there was a dire scenario to be predicted, it was a safe bet that the *Daily Mail* would be front page with it. And so it was that the publication was trumpeting a report that the reshoots were not so much simple transitional scenes as they were massive redoes of some of the sex sequences. The report also indicated that there was concerns about the future of possible sequels if the first film did not bring heat.

As Jamie was fond of being in familiar surroundings and among familiar faces, he was at ease during the reshoots, which according to reports consisted of some moments of passion as well as the more mundane sequences. But, perhaps to spin the rising tide of doubt, several publications, including *E*, ran with stories, complete with unknown inside sources, that indicated all was right in the *Fifty Shades* world.

With the *E* story, in particular, noting that, "The company is still editing the film. They are happy with the way things are going. They are shooting fillers, additional material." To what degree the public was believing the stories was up in the air. What was known was that, in a matter of days, Jamie and his family were on their way back to London.

Jamie had heard all the stories surrounding the *Fifty Shades of Grey* reshoots but seemed at ease with it. He would not begin to speculate on the how and why of it all, trusting that the producers and directors had a very good reason. All the talk of lack of chemistry in the original shoot may well have caused him to think about why certain scenes were seemingly being reshot or enhanced. But ultimately he was of a mind that if it helped to make a better film, the extra effort was fine with him.

Jamie finished up some late *The Fall* press by the end of October and would take a few weeks off in November. With the rush of *Fifty Shades of Grey* promotion set to begin before the end of the year, He acknowledged in a *Daily Express* interview that, "I really do need a break." But the reality was that he was spending much of his off time with a more important full time job, being the best husband and father he could possibly be. And by all reports he was quite good at both, turning simple errands into family outings and enjoying the streets of London in the onset of winter.

"Right now I don't need to work, if there's nothing I want to do" Jamie told *The Guardian* at the time. "I've done three jobs back to back. Let's see how they are received. If there's nothing I want to do, I'll just play golf and change nappies."

When pressed by *Shortlist* on the time off, Jamie admitted that 'It's been a fun couple of years but I'm due a break. I've got the next few weeks off and I'm going to enjoy them."

In the meantime, Jamie's second job as the sexiest man on the planet, continued to dog his attempts at being a legitimate actor. More of an aside to his modeling days, Jamie, nevertheless, continued to have to deal with that aspect of his persona. But, for better or worse, the whole 'The Golden Torso' element took a hit, midway through November, when *People Magazine* made its annual Sexiest Man of the Year announcement. Like most honors of this ilk, Sexiest Man of The Year was a flimsy bit of fluffery, designed more to help draw attention to the magazine and to curry favor with celebrities than as a serious honor. Given all that, to the world at large, Jamie was considered a slam dunk for the honor.

But when the announcement was made, more than one pop culture maven expressed their disappointment that the winner of the dubious honor was actor Chris Hemsworth. As for Jamie, he could care less.

Early in December, 2014, the final battle for the hearts and minds of filmgoers was beginning its final lap. The studio was making maximum use of the internet, releasing new, if not always provocative stills as well as new posters from the film. Late in December the first news of any consequence regarding the long speculated *Fifty Shades of Grey* movie soundtrack was announced when the first single, *Earned It* by The Weekend, was dropped and immediately went top ten on iTunes. The song, reportedly a major element to an erotically charged sex scene from the film, was the perfect tease for the upcoming album which would include music by Beyoncé, Rita Ora and others.

To this point the trailers and photos had given each of the two stars their fair share of attention. But slowly but surely, and perhaps on an unconscious level, the scales seem to be tilting every so slightly in Jamie's direction. In the all- important public's mind, the raw, piercing sexuality of Christian seemed to be winning out over Anastasia's doe-eyed innocence.

Part of that may well have had something to do with the fact that while Dakota had been quite busy in the wake of *Fifty Shades*, she had now retreated to a fairly low public profile while Jamie continued to work throughout the year and was seemingly more amenable to doing press. An example of this tendency to feature Christian was evident in late November when the film's publicity arm trotted out a series of photos highlighting the actors who portrayed Christian's immediate family while, at least to this point, no such release had been done on behalf of Anastasia's family.

Jamie was prepared for a couple of months of promotions, various premieres and more interviews than he could shake a stick at. He had already seen what the mere mention of *Fifty Shades of Grey* could do in media circles and he was already gearing up for the avalanche of hype that was already beginning to gather force. Jamie was more amused at the prospect of massive, last minute publicity than exhausted. After all this was part of the job.

But by early November he had already returned to Vancouver, this time to begin filming on *The 9th Life of Louis Drax* which, perhaps to capitalize on Jamie's notoriety, had accelerated the start of production to late October. For Jamie, it would prove to be an important next step, playing a psychologist in search of a fantastic truth. The role was far removed from anything he had done to date and challenged him with playing a dedicated, somewhat upper class character. Jamie told The Vancouver Sun that the lure was "the mystery and the thrills."

And depending on when it was released, *The 9th Life of Louis Drax* would also give audiences who by that time will have satiated themselves on Jamie as Christian Grey, another outlet for their addiction to all things Jamie. Jamie understood that it all boiled down to how the film was marketed but he also knew that *The 9th Life of Louis Drax* would definitely benefit from having *Fifty Shades of Grey* as its lead in.

While post *Fifty Shades of Grey* projects were keeping him busy and his learning the ropes as both husband and father were a definite part of his day-to-day life, he was never far from the mania that was constantly bubbling to the surface. Jamie was more than willing to do interviews, especially on The second season of *The Fall* which was continuing to draw massive numbers and encouraging reviews, he would become visibly frustrated when the press briefings would predictably turn to whatever bits and pieces of information they could pry from the actor on *Fifty Shades*. Jamie would be apologetic at those moments, especially when he had to repeat the mantra that he was contractually and otherwise sworn to secrecy on most aspects of the film.

"What can I say?," he told *The Guardian*. "It's a big studio and there's big pressure. It's just all a bit silly the way it works. Sometimes I think I could lose my mind."

CHAPTER TWENTY ONE
NOW YOU SEE IT

The sudden drought of legitimate Jamie news hit in early December. With so little day to day news surrounding Jamie to report, the 'silly season' could not have been far behind.

First out of the box, as reported by several tabloid outlets including *Come On!*, was the report that Jamie was spotted walking down the street alone and in a sexy sweater. The report surmised that because Jamie was walking down the street alone, he and Amelia had to be separated and on the road to divorce. People were standing in line to laugh this one off as rubbish and the story became that the story was rubbish.

Not quite as unbelievable but still pretty much filler was the informal internet poll of who should be considered to play James Bond after the news broke that the current Bond, Daniel Craig, has indicated that he will quit playing the super spy after the movie currently filming. Much was made of the fact that Jamie was on the list and that he would make the ideal Bond. End of story.

In late December Jamie, according to a piece in The Inquisitor, would take some heat from certain factions of the bondage and S&M community who had taken exception to the tone of his remarks regarding his research for his role of Christian. It was reported that certain S&M practitioners were not happy with Jamie's dismissive tone and attitude toward their sexual preferences and they charged that his remarks about having to wash before touching his wife and child after witnessing an S&M session were the equivalent of a homophobic slur. Jamie had no comment to the charges.

By December 13, Jamie was putting the finishing touches on *The 9th Life of Louis Drax* and to celebrate the occasion, according to *Just Jared*, Jamie tweeted a picture of himself wandering around the set dressed down in a Stanford University T-shirt with the caption, "I just finished the most beautiful movie I have ever done."

Jamie barely had time to return to London when the press, specifically *The Sun* and *The Independent*, were trumpeting the fact that director Guy Ritchie was actively pursuing Jamie to star as King Arthur in his upcoming film *Knights of the Round Table: King Arthur*, reportedly the first of what would hopefully become a multi film franchise. Jamie was reportedly eager to take on this iconic role but there was a slight fly in the ointment. Jamie had just signed a three-picture deal with Universal on the strength of his *Fifty Shades* performance and the consensus was that there would be two more *Fifty Shades of Grey* films. The stories indicated that Jamie's US agents were hard at work trying to figure out a way for the actor to do both franchises.

This latest announcement was adding fuel to the

fire of speculation that Jamie, indeed, was inclined to strike while the iron was hot in accepting a slew of high profile offers prior to the release of *Fifty Shades of Grey*. But most likely it was Jamie's traditional values that were guiding the actor. As what he considered the importance of the alpha male as being the breadwinner, with a wife and child to support, it was finally a matter of Jamie doing, instinctively, what he would normally do under any circumstance.

Which was to work.

By late December the long predicted rush of *Fifty Shades* hype began in earnest with Jamie and his co-star Dakota leading the charge. People was first out of the box with a *Fifty Shades* cover and inside feature. *Elle UK* also hit the ground running with an exclusive sneak peek of their February 2015 with Jamie, shirtless and flashing biceps, on the cover and an interview and more Jamie beefcake inside. The snippet *Elle UK* released as a tease to the world got the expected internet play with its tale of Jamie visiting a sex dungeon in preparation for his *Fifty Shades'* role. The consensus in publishing circles was that there would be quite a few one shot Fifty Shades of Grey magazines on the stands over the coming weeks.

Jamie and Dakota would also find themselves caught up in the rush of *Fifty Shades of Grey* merchandizing with stylized pictures of the pair promoting *Fifty Shades of Grey* makeup and nail polish. Jamie most likely looked at that element of promotion with a tinge of mortification but, with his modeling background, he knew that tie ins were a part of the promotion game and so he was a good sport about it all. Which was just as well because when Vintage decided to re-release *Fifty Shades of Grey* to coincide with the film's release they slapped a still from the movie on the cover. Realistically movie tie-in books rarely have huge publishing numbers but with the mania for the film growing, it was a safe bet that even those who had multiple copies of all the books would be lining up for this one.

Jamie had been too busy being a husband and father and beginning his post *Fifty Shades of Grey* professional life to keep up on all the news and gossip surrounding his much-anticipated turn as Christian Grey. But with the Christmas season approaching and the release of the film only two months away, he began paying a bit more attention.

"I'll be pretty busy with *Fifty Shades of Grey* until the movie comes out in February," he told *Red Carpet News* reporter Megan Mackay at a charity event in December. "After the movie comes out then I'll be hiding under a rock until the next chapter in my life begins."

It was at that point when he was notified that *Fifty Shades of Grey* would have its world premiere, a select screening for the cast and crew and studio notables, on February 9, 2015 at an as yet undisclosed location in Hollywood. The screening, along with a star studded post screening party, was being talked up as Jamie and Dakota's official coming out in the US.

The pressure was mounting in the film industry and even those who quietly hoped *Fifty Shades* would be a colossal bomb had to realistically hope for it to be a monster hit. Because the reality was that one studio's film failed, it directly impacted the entire industry in terms of what types of films might be made in the future, how much money would be spent and, perhaps most importantly, how US made films might ultimately fare in the all -important international market.

And so it would be the international market, considered by many insiders where the biggest share of the profit would be made, who would end up making an even bigger splash on February 11 when Jamie, Dakota, director Sam Taylor Johnson and EL James would be on hand for the first international screening of *Fifty Shades of Grey* at the Berlin Film Festival. Film journalists immediately speculated that premiering *Fifty Shades* in at the prestigious Berlin Film Festival was actually a more calculating than spontaneous decision. Whether they wanted it or not, *Fifty Shades of Grey* had garnered the majority of its media interest based on the more erotic and explicit moments of the storyline. By showing the film in Berlin, whose festival was noted for its more intellectual and artistic leanings, they were hoping that *Fifty Shades of Grey* would ultimately emerge as the serious film the filmmakers had always intended it to be.

Jamie, in particular, was looking forward to the Berlin festival because this would be pretty up a traditional unveiling, replete with red carpet appearances, endless photos and interviews and, perhaps most importantly, the first time critics would get to see the film.

For Jamie, Berlin would be the end of a very long journey…And the beginning of yet another.

Jamie knew how off base those comments were. The response to one film was not going to make or break him. There had been ten long, hard years leading up to this moment. In his own laidback way, Jamie would tell anyone who cared to listen that he had long ago earned this special moment in entertainment history. That fans had been speculating for a good two years about how he would come across and, to satisfy their fantasies, what state of dress or undress the reality would be. More than 100 million people had bought into the fantasy of *Fifty Shades of Grey*. Now the pressure was truly on.

Could Jamie deliver?

Jamie's co-star on *The Fall*, Anderson, has always been quick with the good-natured barbs and, with Jamie present, she addressed the speculation on the fate of *Fifty Shades* in a conversation with Newsbeat.com when she joshed "The movie hasn't even come out yet! He might suck!"

It was all good fun and Jamie, the always reliable good sport, took it that way. But it would be a gross understatement to say that an untold number of studio executives and bottom line bean counters had their fingers crossed as the days until *Fifty Shades of Grey*'s official unveiling counted down to the low double digits.

But finally it remained for the quite circumspect Jamie to address his *Fifty Shades of Grey* future.

"I'm not fearful of *Fifty Shades of Grey*," he told *GQ UK*. "I'm not really fearful of that stuff at all. It's just work. It's strange work to be sure but it's still just work…"

…"I just get on with it."

FILMOGRAPHY

FILM
THE SIEGE OF JADOTVILLE (2015)
THE 9TH LIFE OF LOUIS DRAX (2015)
ADAM JONES (2015)
FIFTY SHADES OF GREY (2015)
FLYING HOME (2014)
SHADOWS IN THE SUN ((2009)
NICE TO MEET YOU (2008)
BEYOND THE RAVE (2008)
MARIE ANTOINETTE (2006)

TELEVISION
NEW WORLDS (2014)
THE FALL (2013-PRESENT)
ONCE UPON A TIME (2011-2013)

DISCOGRAPHY
SONS OF JIM
EP'S
FAIRYTALE (2005)
MY BURNING SUN (2006)

SINGLES
FAIRYTALE (2005)
MY BURNING SUN (2006)

SOURCES

MAGAZINES

ASOS, Glamour Poland, In!, Red, Entertainment Weekly, Shortlist, British Vogue, The Journal, Out, Mode, The Stage, ES, Hello, Elle, Glamour, Interview, Fangoria, In Style, Grazia Italy, Esquire UK, GQ UK, Watch, Heat, Variety, Stylist,

WEBSITES

J.P. Watson.com, News Letter.com, Now Daily.com, This Is London.com, Mr. Porter.com, Fabulous.com, Now.com, Radio Times.com, Glamour Chick.com, Yahoo Movies.com, Bang Showbiz.com, WENN.com, Celebrities Worldwide.com, What's On TV.com, Just Jared.com, Boston.com, Stupid Celebrities.com, Jamie Dornan Life.com, E News.com, Digital Spy.com, Entertainmentwise.com, Red Carpet News.com, AsiaOne.com, Huffington Post UK.com. BBC.com, O Canada.com, Fifty Shades World.com, Newsbeat.com

NEWSPAPERS

The Sunday Times, The Scotsman, The Telegraph, Irish News, The Sun, Belfast Telegraph, The Times, The Daily Record, The Evening Standard, The New York Times, Variety, Chicago Tribune, The

Hollywood Reporter, The Sun, The Guardian, The Observer, Herts & Essex Observer, The Sunday World, Daily Express, The Vancouver Sun, The Daily Mirror, The Evening Herald, The Independent.

TELEVISION

The Today Show, Ten News, The Graham Norton Show, Extra

MISCELLANEOUS

San Diego Comic Con (presentation), Flying Home (production notes), An Evening In The Writer's Room (television series), The Fall (press junket), 50 Shades blog.

For more books by Marc Shapiro visit
https://riverdaleavebooks.com/

The Secret Life of EL James: The Unauthorized Biography
https://riverdaleavebooks.com/books/16/the-secret-life-of-el-james

We Love Jenni: The Unauthorized Biography of Jenni Rivera with Charlie Vazquez
https://riverdaleavebooks.com/books/28/we-love-jenni-an-unauthorized-biography

Who Is Katie Holmes?: The Unauthorized Biography
https://riverdaleavebooks.com/books/33/who-is-katie-holmes-an-unauthorized-biography

Legally Bieber: Justin Bieber at 18
The Unauthorized Biography
http://riverdaleavebooks.com/books/41/legally-bieber-justin-bieber-at-18

Annette Funicello: America's Sweetheart
The Unauthorized Biography
http://riverdaleavebooks.com/books/44/annette-funicello-americas-sweetheart

Game: The Resurrection of Tim Tebow
The Unauthorized Biography
http://riverdaleavebooks.com/books/3084/game-the-resurrection-of-tim-tebow

Lorde: Your Heroine
How This Young Feminist Broke the Rules and Succeeded
http://riverdaleavebooks.com/books/4113/lorde-your-heroine-how-this-young-feminist-broke-the-rules-and-succeeded

ABOUT THE AUTHOR

Marc Shapiro is the *NY Times* best-selling author of *J.K. Rowling: The Wizard Behind Harry Potter*, *Justin Bieber: The Fever!* and many other best-selling celebrity biographies. He has been a free-lance entertainment journalist for more than twenty-five years, covering film, television, and music for a number of national and international newspapers and magazines. He has just finished *The Real Steele: The Unauthorized Biography of Dakota Johnson* and *Inside Grey's Anatomy: The Unauthorized Biography* of Jamie Dornan for Riverdaleavebooks.com.

Printed in Great Britain
by Amazon